Ruminations on Foggy Mornings

Ruminations on Foggy Mornings

An Anthology of Short Essays Exploring the Conundrums facing Contemporary Society

Supriya Pattanayak

AUTHORSPRESS

Worldwide Circulation through Authorspress Global Network
First Published in 2021
by
Authorspress
Q-2A Hauz Khas Enclave, New Delhi-110 016 (India)
Phone: (0) 9818049852
E-mail: authorspressgroup@gmail.com
Website: www.authorspressbooks.com

Ruminations on Foggy Mornings
ISBN 978-93-90588-03-9

Printed in India at Thomson Press (India) Limited

For my Parents

Contents

Preface

The year 2020 has been a defining year for humanity. It will probably be best remembered for the Covid-19 pandemic, although it was also the year of severe environmental disasters like the bushfires of Australia or the orange sky of California. It will also be remembered for testing the human ability to adapt and our resilience in the face of unprecedented circumstances. It was a watershed year for change, change through the rise in many forms of social activism and social awakening, change defined by an eventful US presidential election leading to a woman Vice-President with many firsts or change in the global geo-political order.

Yet, I believe, personally we will remember it to be the year that forced all of us to pause mid-step from our hectic lives and spend a lot of time confined in our homes. So while a tiny virus crippled economies and ground the world to a halt, both literally and figuratively, to such an extent that even the earth's surface vibrations quietened down to record levels, while it has given us more stress, be it physical, mental, familial and/or financial, it has also given us the gift of time, for ourselves. It has forced us to sit in our homes and take a long hard look at our life choices. Choices, that led to defining our lives as an individual, as a family, as a society and as humanity. It has brought the long-term problems facing us individually and collectively to the forefront, those that were pushed to the background, due to our immediate short-term issues and our busy schedule.

In this Anthropocene age, 2020 was marked as the year when manmade materials finally outweighed all living things on earth. It was also the year our earth and its environment gave us a warning and forced us to take heed of the seemingly gradual yet rapid changes we are causing around us, and its consequences.

I believe the pause has led us to shift focus from the here and now to the when and then, to inspect and introspect on the greater issues surrounding us, be it the natural disasters caused by climate change, the structural racism and the social divisions that we took for granted or even the power of social media and its pros and cons which have been highlighted in this altered world.

Almost all of mankind lived in some form of isolation and social distancing, be it immediate or international, and predominantly connected virtually, during 2020. We spent our time working from home and keeping in touch with our loved ones through video calls, so much so that we coined a new term for it, "Zoom fatigue".

However, we have a great need to connect with others beyond our immediate family. To satisfy the itch and to beat the claustrophobia and associated depression due to loneliness, we now engage actively in the happenings of society and take a stand on the issues facing it. This has resulted in triggering many social changes, which otherwise would have been less powerful, less mainstream and definitely less impactful. We stay connected with the world by looking at the problems staring us in the face and try to find a way of contributing our own 1/12th of a teaspoon, for the betterment of our society.

Over the months, I made an attempt to capture the conundrums we face as part of our daily life, in the form of opinion pieces for an Indian newspaper *Odishabytes*. It resulted in this collection of essays that are not just topical but also explores our choices and takes a stab at how we could, potentially, help contribute towards them.

Please excuse the liberties I have taken by generalising as "we" and "us". The opinions expressed are purely mine, unless quoted otherwise. The aim is not to direct anyone to behave in a certain way but to ignite the process of contemplation in the readers' minds, through thought-provoking questions. It is then left to the readers, to decide for themselves what is their stand on these issues and how they would like to contribute towards it, if ever. Whether we agree or disagree on a topic, I sincerely hope it will kindle a deliberation in your mind, occasionally funny but often on matters of grave significance. Meanwhile, I hope you enjoy reading them.

Supriya Pattanayak

Dear NEOWISE

The Comet NEOWISE was within 64.3 million miles of earth in July 2020, close enough that we were able to see it with our naked eye or with simple binoculars. Almost the entire world spent a few nights staring into the sky, trying to catch a glimpse of the celestial body. Perhaps if it was a living being or had life on it, we could have had a conversation with it, probably along these lines.

Dear NEOWISE,
What's the news?
Hope you are fine,
not having blues.

We are very excited,
to speak to you.
To make things easier,
have named you too.

There are a few things,
we want to comprehend.
Where do you come from?
Have you visited beforehand?

Although earth has existed
for billions of years,
we have just evolved,
so, we won't know for sure.

Celestial bodies rarely come,
this close to us.
Apparently, one hit and
destroyed our dinosaurs.

Why did you come here?
Were you also just curious?
Did you get called by the sun,
or serve another purpose?

Anyway, please don't mind
our prying and be shy.
It's lovely to watch you,
adorning our night sky.

Visiting us from beyond
the snow line, far away.
Have you met anyone
like us, along the way?

You carry the mystery in,
your rocks, ice and dust,
but a holiday into the tropics,
is really burning you up.

The steam you let off,
as our sun roasts you,
Leaves an exquisite trail,
while you pass through.

We try to catch a glimpse,
filled with wonder,
For you look beautiful,
So, we just admire.

We hope and try
to travel far into space,
so, may call on you,
or your other associates.

Else if we manage to
survive and mature,
learn to balance
progress with nature.

We will meet on
your next trip here,
seven millenniums
into our distant future.

Have a safe journey
back to your terrain.
So long, adieu,
till we meet again.

Words are things. You must be careful, careful about calling people out of their names, using racial pejoratives and sexual pejoratives and all that ignorance. Don't do that. Someday we'll be able to measure the power of words. I think they are things. They get on the walls. They get in your wallpaper. They get in your rugs, in your upholstery, and your clothes, and finally into you.

— Maya Angelou

1. What's in a Name? A Lot it seems

Juliet: "What's in a name? That which we call a rose by any other name would smell as sweet." – Shakespeare's Romeo and Juliet, Act II. Scene II

When you have a name like Juliet, you can speak but for the rest of us, we have to make do with what our parents have named us. It is part of our identity.

If you have an easy to pronounce name, like say Ramesh in India or John in the West, great. An easy on the tongue, cross-culture name is even better. A name that can be abbreviated to something short and sweet like a Sid for Sidharth, is ultimate, as it ticks all the boxes both in India and across the world.

But what if you have a name like "X Æ A-Xii"? That, as you may know, is the name of Elon Musk, CEO of Tesla & SpaceX and his musician partner Grimes' newborn son. Originally named "X Æ A-12", the name was deemed illegal under Californian law, because it contained characters that are not in the modern English alphabet and was then changed to "X Æ A-Xii".

They may both be famous in their own rights, but they have definitely ensured their son is even more so, just by giving him a promethean name.

The world is going crazy, trying to figure out how to pronounce it. If their own tweets and subsequent news reports are to be believed, the parents themselves disagree over it too.

Despite the avant-garde name, he may not be in the minority regarding difficulty in nomenclature pronunciation. I recently met a girl named "Áine" from Ireland and was struggling to pronounce it, till she helpfully said its "on-yah". As with many other Irish names like Aoife (EE-fe/Eva) or Siobhan (shi-VAWN), the spelling and pronunciation differ. Unless you are told or you have googled, it is hard to know the correct way.

This goes for names in other cultures too, like a J in Spanish is actually pronounced as H, so a Jose is actually called "Hose". However, these are all cultural aspects, a onetime problem and not actually a personal choice.

Other cultures like in Cantonese-speaking Hong Kong or even in Mandarin-speaking mainland China and Taiwan, people adopt a Westernised name while starting school or later. It is rarely reflected in legal documents but is widely used by the person to identify himself. It could be done to overcome a hard to pronounce native name, a colonial hangover in Hong Kong or simply to borrow an identity and in turn the Western interpersonal communication system which is quite different from the strict Chinese one. Most people choose a name that closely matches their original one, say Kitty for the Chinese symbol Kit but others pick random ones like Jack, December or even Rolex.

On the other hand, there are names that sound inherently funny. Comedian Amy Schumer and her chef husband Chris Fischer changed their son's middle name from Gene Attell Fischer to Gene David Fischer after a year. They realised Gene Attell can rhyme with "Genital" and they did not want him to be bullied for it. Well, some children are not so fortunate and get bullied for much less, despite their parents' best intentions.

I sat next to one Harshit ("harr-shi-tt" meaning joyful in Hindi), while on a plane to the US and he was regaling me with his naming woes. Harshit being difficult to pronounce for an average American, when he shortened it to "Harsh" people asked him why such a sweet boy was called "harsh", as in cruel. He could not go with "shit", for obvious reasons. In the end people ended up calling him Harry just for the sake of convenience but of course, his parents were not amused.

An acquaintance from Hong Kong was called Seven. When I queried, he explained that he had actually chosen the name Steven as a child when he started school, but he did not know how to spell it so ended up with Seven and never changed it.

Sometimes we also think people look like their names. Actually, it is part of the well-researched social Bouba/Kiki effect[1] published in 2001. It says, if you have a round face then people assign a soft "round" sounding name (Bouba) and if you have a sharp angular face then people assign a sharp sounding name (Kiki).

In fact, this theory carries on further. We generally have a mild subconscious bias for people whose names match their faces. If a face shape does not conform to the name it can lead to social implications like not liking or trusting someone or can even go further as not to vote for them in an election.

It makes me wonder which category X Æ A-Xii will fall under though. Will calling someone "X Ash A 12", and I am taking a stab at it here, negate the effect or make it more prominent?

Whether the name matches the face or they have never been bullied for it, most people like their own names. I was in the minority who hate their names and have always complained about it to parents. However, after going through these experiences, I am just relieved I can at least write my name using the twenty six English alphabets and people can, mostly, pronounce it correctly.

---

1   https://en.wikipedia.org/wiki/Bouba/kiki_effect

Meanwhile the majority of parents are still trying to name kids with something that is short, sweet and easy on a multilingual tongue, unlike Elon Musk and Grimes.

Who knows, like their respective scientific and musical innovations, this may lead to a new trend in futuristic names too and result in a change in government naming rules itself. They may yet have the last laugh and only time will tell.

❖❖❖

Do not judge, or you too will be judged. For in the same way you judge others, you will be judged, and with the measure you use, it will be measured to you.

– Matthew 7.1-2

2. Cancel Culture: Mob Mentality or Mob Power?

One of the most powerful trends to sweep social media in the last few years is "Cancel culture". Packed with the collective power of no-bodies it wields the power of a mob to force changes.

Cancel culture refers to the act of cancelling or boycotting an individual or organisation, based on what they have spoken or how they have acted, which is deemed objectionable to a large section of people.

It can largely be credited for helping amplify the changes of the #metoo movement and the current racial discussion, among others, by providing a platform to millions of collective voices and bring about changes in the society.

In both instances individuals who felt powerless in the presence of formidable figures or the establishment, expressed their anger via social media and forced them to take remedial action. Even a dominant movie mogul like Harvey Weinstein was forced to face consequences of his actions, mainly due to the effect of cancel culture.

Considering its part in the #metoo movement, it is ironic that the first use of cancel was misogynistic when in a 1991 movie called New Jack City, the gangster Nino Brown called for his girlfriend to be cancelled saying "Cancel that b****." Although Lil Wayne referenced it in 2010 as part of a song, the trend caught on in social media after a reality show Love and Hip-Hop: New York used it in a fight where a character called out to his love interest, you are cancelled. By 2015, the origin had become irrelevant and it was widely used across the world to express disapproval for something or someone.

At its heart is the idea that people who have helped make careers of some, have given them power and money also have the power to take it all away, if the person concerned does not conform to certain ideas.

It is also about holding people accountable to what they say or have said, sometimes years ago. Kevin Hart faced a backlash in 2019 for his old homophobic tweets in 2011. It made him step down as the Oscar host.

Harry Potter author, J.K. Rowling recently faced cancelling for speaking about her outdated views on transgenders. It may be too early to say what effect it will have on her as social media may not have enough power to make any difference to her or maybe she does not care.

In the case of celebrities, who depend on the power of social media, they lose social currency and are financially effected. If powerful, they have enough support to ride it through and many do not face long-term effects. Cancelling of Karan Johar and others associated with the Hindi film industry, as a reaction to nepotism claims in the Sushant Singh Rajput case may not have a long-term effect for them.

Kevin Hart is also an example to show the limitations of the cancel culture. Although it caused him damage in the short run, it did not end his career in the long term. He is back to making money and performing to house full audiences.

However, cancel culture may not be as innocuous as it sounds. If overdone it can be seen as a form of cyber bullying. People are tried and hanged before they even have a chance to respond, and if in the wrong ask for forgiveness or even make amends. It can also be instigated or amplified by others, to settle old scores.

The impact of cancelling is more severe at an individual level where friends can gang up and boycott a person. It causes the person being cancelled to feel lonely and socially cut off. It can be traumatic and can lead to depression and even suicide. However, are these people really friends? How strong is a friendship if they can turn against you at the drop of a hat? Most in person friends would allow us to speak our mind and if in the wrong seek forgiveness and a second chance.

Cancel culture, if not moderated may lead to a society where there is no place for evolution of ideas or alternate viewpoints being discussed.

Even newspapers, traditionally a space where everyone has a say have not been spared. James Bennet, a senior editor at the *New York Times*, resigned amid a furious backlash over the newspaper's publication of a controversial and unfiltered comment piece penned by a Republican Senator.

Post this over 150 writers and public figures, including J.K. Rowling and Salman Rushdie signed and published an open letter in *Harper's magazine* calling out "Cancel culture" for stifling free speech. They said it creates an atmosphere where people fear speaking their minds or expressing alternate opinions, expecting severe repercussions. While their motives have been questioned and maybe debatable, we cannot deny that cancel culture leads to a very narrow conformist view of life. It is a case of either you are with the mob or get crushed by it.

The aim should be to find a balanced space where everyone can speak their minds and have a healthy debate. We should be able to draw a line between calling out someone from bullying them.

We must of course use social media to express our opinions, to react by aligning ourselves with what we think is right. It is a unique power that we can use for the benefit of society. It gives us the ability to hand out social justice through a social platform by society itself. However, we must fact check and differentiate between cancelling someone from threatening them.

It would be advisable to bear in mind the words of former US President Barack Obama who said that easy social media judgments do not amount to true social activism. Speaking at the Obama Foundation Summit, former US President Barack Obama said: "The cancel culture is predicated on this idea of purity; the illusion that you're never compromised, and you're always politically 'woke' and all that stuff. You should get over that quickly. The world is messy, there are ambiguities. People who do really good stuff have flaws. People who you are fighting may love their kids. And share certain things with you."

The idea of Cancel Culture is to hold people accountable for their actions, past or present and give them a chance to make amends. The idea is most certainly not to act out a vendetta against anyone who dares transgress against the views you hold.

I was outraged, yes, but that was only the beginning of a process in which my heart completely defeated my rational judgment. I accepted all the claims retailed by the media as facts, and I repeated them as if I were being paid for it.

— Edward Snowden, *Permanent Record*

3. Computational Propaganda:
The Invisible Threat

We live in a connected world as part of a cyber space where our lives are being chronicled through our online activity, especially on our mobile phones. Market research firm techARC, said in its report that India had 502.2 million smartphone users as of December 2019. This means over 77 per cent of Indians are now accessing wireless broadband through smartphones.

While it means people have the ability to connect and access information, it also means that being human they will react to it. In the process they are creating a digital wealth of information through millions of likes, clicks, posts, tweets and shopping habits. With the rapid growth in Big Data, these are not just stored but also analysed in seconds.

Companies regularly troll through the internet to evaluate reaction and trends so they can respond, to ensure success. An example could be the launch of a new product, a movie release or even the response to an announcement by a major company.

One of the most visible uses of this is probably in politics. Politicians, quick to identify an opportunity, jumped on to social media platforms and used it to their advantage. The ability to reach out to millions of people without actually spending huge amounts of effort, time and money, is changing the landscape of politics. It also means content is important and needs to be right the first time as it moves fast and can neither be controlled nor modified. Hence, they use information to analyse and gauge the mood of the public towards any given situation and then try to deliver the right response.

If this data is used for people's benefit, it is to be applauded. On the other hand, if this is being used for manipulating people and furthering political or ideological self-interests, it turns into computational propaganda.

The term computational propaganda literally means information, especially of a biased or misleading nature, used to promote or publicise a particular political cause or point of view.

The 2016 presidential elections or the Brexit vote are some of the best examples of it. Cambridge Analytica harvested the data of millions of Facebook users, profiled them and ran targeted campaigns to influence them to vote a certain way. Although both CA and FB were exposed and faced repercussions, it showed the fallacies of sharing data on social media and led to tightening of data protection.

However, it did not stop the march of computational propaganda. Today it is widely acknowledged that individuals, countries or organisations use Artificial Intelligence (AI) Bots to influence and drive public opinion towards their agenda which could be political, racial or even ideological.

Various groups engage these AI Bots to troll the internet and drive forward a particular point of view by spreading disinformation through liking or commenting on posts and tweets in thousands, if not millions. They help create and market "fake news".

The social media companies like Twitter, Facebook and Google are being accused of not doing enough to fight them. Facebook lost around 56 billion of market value in June, as large companies pulled out ads, citing it's failing to sufficiently categorise and mark hate speech and fight disinformation across it's platforms. With an aim to maintain a balance between free speech versus hate speech, Mark Zuckerberg has said they will start labelling posts rather than removing them.

So how do we fight an unknown enemy? For now, tech companies are aiming to fight fire with fire, so fight AI with more AI. The idea is to use Artificial Intelligence and Machine Learning to pick up and fact check things, before allowing it to be posted. Essentially, we use good AI to identify the rogue bots spreading misinformation and stop their activity.

But who defines "good"? The important point is that Artificial Intelligence is just that, artificial. It reflects the thoughts of the humans, who create and manage them. For example, whether Brexit is good or bad, it depends on who you ask.

The more pertinent question is should we leave this fight to a handful of tech leaders and their teams? Can we depend on them to have the best interests of humanity in their hearts instead of their share price and returns? Zuckerberg was forced to act owing to heavy reaction from FB employees and loss of wealth for his company and himself. More importantly why should they decide what is positive or negative for us?

Computational propaganda is the probably the biggest threat we face to our democracies and our freedom to choose without being influenced, across the world. We face psychological warfare, in the cyber world, from an invisible enemy.

On the one hand we have a handful of powerful people trying to brainwash us to align with their thought process. On the other, we depend on a few businessmen to prevent it from happening.

Although it could be one of many strategies, maybe that is not enough. Maybe we should look at a coordinated global effort from non-profit organisations to counter it. Maybe there are other ways we need to come up with in this ever-changing world. Some serious thought needs to be given to it.

Whatever the future strategy, ultimately the onus is on us to be able to question everything we read, fact check them and make an unbiased decision, from our individual perspective. Only this can help prevent us from being manipulated and will help preserve our freedom of thought and our way of life.

These fragments I have shored against my ruins
                     — T.S. Eliot, The Waste Land and Other Poems

4. A Shot of Nostalgia for the Soul

It was a weekday, so a phone call from my parents mid-morning surprised me. By the time the call ended my heart had turned heavy, for I had lost an elderly relative to natural causes. The knowledge that we could neither visit to pay our last respects nor physically comfort the immediate family made us feel dejected, as sometimes a phone or video call does not cut it.

I felt sadness but the most overwhelming emotion I felt was intense nostalgia. I spent some time over the next few days thinking about my past interactions and relived some fond memories.

I was not overly surprised at my reaction though, for lately I seem to be dwelling on the past a lot. In fact, we all seem to be ruminating about days gone by and looking towards the past rather than the future, during this unusual lockdown phase.

How often have we caught ourselves rummaging through old pictures and sometimes posting them on social media sites? Most of us like listening to old songs, from our teenage days, which have joyful connotations of a carefree life spent with loved ones. Others spend time cooking or baking delicacies. I have had regular catch ups with school and college friends or anyone with whom I share some pleasant memories, over the last few months, with most of the conversation dwelling on the past.

Under normal circumstances we all feel a mild version of nostalgia at certain times of our lives, like during stress, loss or anxiety. An example could be seeing people waiting in hospital corridors lost in happy memories spent with the patient, which at other times they would have barely remembered.

We may pin it down to having more time now, which although true, is only part of the reason. Now, the feeling is much more intense and is being experienced by almost everyone. The question to consider is, why do we feel this way and does it have any adverse effect on our mental health?

The word was originally coined in the 17th century by a medical student Johannes Hofer, to describe the intense feeling of melancholy, considered a negative feeling then, he observed in Swiss mercenaries fighting away from home. By the late 20th century research had changed it into being considered a positive emotion, with its main function being to maintain a coherent narrative or a link between the past and the present, when there are rapid changes in life, planned or unplanned.

Nostalgia is a perfectly normal physiological reaction to the stress we are currently experiencing. Previously the travel time to and from office used to be our way of getting mentally prepared for work and switching off later. Now as we work from home, with both a laptop and a pile of dirty dishes or laundry visible, we cannot mentally break away from either home or office and it creates stress. So, we may feel nostalgic about the demarcation, our travel time, as we crave that clean break.

It could be our way of handling the unpredictability surrounding us by countering it with the known and the definite, that cannot be changed. The social distancing measures have made us lonely by confining us to our homes. We feel powerless over our present and our future, as we can plan for neither.

Compounding the issue are the lost memories, the ones we cannot build. Millions will miss out on creating the memories of graduating from school or college, saying goodbye or having farewell parties, previously taken for granted by everyone.

Nostalgia helps our brain recreate the sense of control we once had, in the absence of any new ones being made in the present.

These negative emotions cause an increasing amount of depression, among the population. A feeling of melancholy comes from the seemingly perpetual negativity in the media and fear of losing things close to us, like our loved ones, career, financial security or even just our way of life.

Nostalgia filled with happy memories, is our minds coping mechanism to help us stay balanced, keep us company and ward away negativity. It ultimately helps us get a sense of optimism for the future.

Nostalgia is a very social emotion and generally involves loved ones and cherished relationships. It is a way of comforting us by remembering the enjoyable time spent with our loved ones, so bringing us physiologically closer to them, even though physically distanced now.

It helps us get reassurance from our past and gives us a sense of self-worth. It reminds us of the events that shaped us, reminds us of who we really are and that we have not changed under these trying circumstances.

So next time you feel like listening to an old song and travelling down the memory lane, be self-indulgent. Let your mind wander back to more congenial times and get a shot of much needed positivity.

Just make sure to steer clear of any bad ones and it might just be the magic portion recommended to help fight the despair around and keep you sane.

❖ ❖ ❖

Cherish the natural world because you are part of it and you depend on it.

— Sir David Attenborough

5. Humans vs Animals: A Lose-Lose Battle

Do you know what is the hottest makeup trend for summer 2020? "Dolphin skin" look. Yes, giving the impression of having a wet, slippery and silky-smooth skin like that of a dolphin, using makeup tricks, is the latest craze. It has a number of high-profile fans from supermodel Bella Hadid to reality TV star Kim Kardashian.

Isn't it ironic that we see this beauty trend start around the same time as the Dolphin hunting season ends? The Taiji's Dolphin drive hunt lasts over six months in Japan mainly from September till about March. During the 2019/2020 season alone over 560 Dolphins were slaughtered while hundreds more were captured or accidentally killed.

Humans adore nature and look for beauty in it but also make every effort to tame it for entertainment, use it for benefits or even kill and eat it to the point of extinction.

With the increase in world population and change in food habits the pressure for food, especially protein, is increasing at a pace where demand outstrips supply. This leads us to engage in deforestation, unsustainable agricultural practices and wildlife exploitation to fulfil the demand for meat. People eat all types of animals, domestic and wild, to satisfy their protein needs. The belief that human life is superior to animal or plant life drives us to do it guilt free.

With advancements in technology, we can control and kill more efficiently while protecting ourselves with biotechnology. For example, improvements in fishing techniques have led to something called bottom trawling. It basically means dragging huge heavy nets across the ocean floor, picking up everything along the way. The fish having commercial use are retained and the bycatch of unprofitable animals and corals are thrown back into the sea. The hurt animals mostly die and the damage to the seafloor is irreplaceable. In the longer term, these selfish actions of humans cause ecological imbalance and biodegradation of natural habitat.

On land, deforestation and illegal wildlife trade leads to the loss of habitat for animals and ultimately endangerment or extinction of species. While the larger impact on climate is focused on, there is less focus on deforestation which subsequently leads to diet changes in the effected population. Studies have clearly shown that with their regular source of fruits and vegetables gone they tend to eat more protein rich diets obtained through processed supermarket meat or from wild animals.

Overtime, this exploitation of nature on both land and at sea, changes the precarious balance between how animals and humans interact and finally backfires in the form of Zoonotic diseases.

Zoonotic disease is a form of disease that transmits from animals to humans. In the last century we have had around six major outbreaks with Ebola and the recent Covid-19 being the latest and the most well-known among them.

It is widely agreed that both came from contact with wild bats, when they were used as food source. In June, a new swine flu strain with potential for turning into a pandemic was discovered among pigs in China.

All this can be traced back to the rise in demand for protein. Meat production has increased significantly in the last 50 years. We no longer think much of tucking into a burger instead of having a home-cooked vegetarian meal. It not only causes health issues but also has a long-term effect on the earth's ecosystem.

With the world population slated to reach nine billion by 2050, it will be impossible to feed it at the current level of protein intake. After consuming all available animals on earth, we will need four more earths for it.

Instead, making slight changes to our food habits will go a long way in not only preserving earth and its biodiversity but also benefit our health. For example, if just the population of the US went meat free one day a week, it would prevent greenhouse gas emissions equal to that produced by all of France and cut the risk of disease by 19 per cent.

Covid-19 has given us a flavour of the large-scale impact that Zoonotic diseases can have. The UN published a report in July 2020, that offers governments strategies on how to prevent future Zoonotic outbreaks through sustainable land management, improving biodiversity and investing in scientific research.

Inger Andersen, Under-Secretary General and Executive Director of the UN Environment Programme has said. "The science is clear that if we keep exploiting wildlife and destroying our ecosystems, then we can expect to see a steady stream of these diseases jumping from animals to humans in the years ahead. To prevent future outbreaks, we must become much more deliberate about protecting our natural environment."

It is unrealistic to expect the entire world to change their food habits and go vegan overnight. However, implementing planned and strict government policy on deforestation, raising awareness among the population about respecting the balance with our natural habitat and taking steps to preserve biodiversity would have a massive positive impact on avoiding any future outbreak of Zoonotic diseases.

Isn't it high time, we think about a global long-term strategy for food consumption and production across the world? If we continue the current trend of mindless exploitation, then our aspiration for Dolphin skin and Cheetah's speed will depend on historical references rather than live examples. Our next generation may never get to see them in real life.

We may end up losing the very nature we love to admire and imitate while the occurrence of novel diseases will increase in frequency and intensity, till life as we know it will be lost forever.

Intelligence is not the ability to store information, but to know where to find it.

— Albert Einstein

6. Tech-Tonic Shift: From Informed Decision-Making to Information Overload

The recent sad and upsetting events around racial discrimination and the subsequent protests have dominated the world stage, even upstaging the pandemic. People's frustrations have grown to the point that they now want to remove visible reminders of the very symbols of imperialism and racism, like statues of people associated with them.

I came across the news about Oxford governors agreeing to work towards removing the statue of colonialist Cecil Rhodes, which remains at Oxford's Oriel College. While I do not want to get into a discussion about the right or wrong of it, what got me interested was the familiarity of the name. The question answered itself when the article mentioned his famous Rhodes scholarship for Oxford.

Having grown up in an academic environment, I had heard about it but for me and the multitude of people, he was just a name. I had no idea of who he was or what he represented, as was the case for many other scholarships named after people. I immediately googled a few others, like Fulbright, to understand why the scholarships had been established.

I wondered why I had never looked it up before? I realised the answer was literally staring at me in the face, my phone. A wealth of knowledge is readily available now, enabled by the connected world of the internet on our laptops and smartphones, which we did not have access to before.

Trying to find out about him would have meant asking someone, who may or may not have known about him or a trip to the massive library to look through the pages of Encyclopedia Britannica, my first point of call for research, as a young person. While google existed, my access to the internet was restrictive and when available very slow. By the time that changed my interest had faded, confined to a distant memory, till now.

The super-fast connectivity and availability of information, literally at our fingertips, is gradually changing our perception and ultimately decisions, regarding our way of life.

Everyone may not be as adept at technology as the latest Generation Alpha, who were born after iPads and iPhones or even the Gen Z who have lived their entire life in a connected world with smartphones as their favourite mode of communication, however they are definitely adapting to it fast and well.

Today, out of habit, every time a question occurs to us, we ask a search engine for the answer, so much so that "googling" has become a verb. The search may be as mundane as the meaning of a word, location or directions for travel or even shop opening times to important background research on a company we wish to join. Sometimes this goes to an extreme where we try to self-diagnose medical conditions without seeking doctors' advice.

A person not found on Facebook/Twitter/Insta is considered a ghost. We are moving towards a stage where a company that has no web presence like an entry in Wiki pages or a LinkedIn profile is easily dismissed.

Information now drives consumer behaviour, and companies in turn. People are conscious of what lies behind the brand too. They want to know if the clothes they buy or food they eat are ethically and sustainably produced. Hiding is no longer an option and is considered a sign of guilt. In fact some companies want to control the narrative in the media and market themselves, by providing information freely. The consumer stands in front of the item, searches for the information and then decides to buy or not, all under sixty seconds.

So in addition to the availability of information, the reach and reaction times are a matter of hours instead of days now. One tweet by Elon Musk about the share price of Tesla being too high, wiped 14billion USD from Tesla's value, overnight.

Of course, information is always welcome but sometimes debatable. I look up maps and chart optimal travel paths for the day, before I visit a new city. I even view the stations or landmarks beforehand on google street view, so as not to get lost or depend on strangers to guide me. This is all in addition to having google maps guiding me dynamically, especially if I am travelling alone, so I can feel secure. However, you could argue that I lose an opportunity to speak and see the place through the eyes of a local or reduce the impact of seeing something for the first time.

Everyone has access to information and hence the decision is also ours to make. I may go with a local guide or random exploring, if I have company or feel safe. A person may buy non-ethical clothing because they love it or even because it is the only thing they can afford. What's certain is that going forward people will do more research and then decide, rather than taking things for granted.

Meanwhile, will the Rhodes scholarship be retained, although I have not read anything to the contrary? It will be even more interesting to see if this will affect the uptake from future students, now that information of his colonial past has been laid bare.

❖❖❖

If you expect nothing from anybody, you're never disappointed.

— Sylvia Plath

7. The Art of Balancing Expectations

A recent conversation with a young cousin made me think about the effect expectations of people around us has on our lives.

He has secured 90 plus per cent and a good university placement but is not keen on pursuing his studies in the new online format with limited in person interactions and would rather take a gap year. However, he was worried about not living up to his parents' expectations and felt he did not have a choice to take a year's break without causing them disappointment. I felt sad hearing him base his decision solely on others' expectations.

We learn to manage expectations between ourselves and those of others early on in life, even as a child and hone the skill over the years. Those who successfully manage to navigate it, learn to reduce disappointment and increase their happiness. Unfortunately, a vast majority of us struggle with it.

It is well-researched that our opinion and behaviour are greatly impacted by our own and others' expectations of us. This is called the expectation effect and can be categorised into a few types.

A positive expectation from others leads to performance improvements is widely acknowledged. An example could be the high expectations of a manager leads to higher productivity from his subordinate or even his whole team. Another example is the academic performance of students increases due to their teachers and parents having high expectations from them. When expectation is conveyed positively, students work hard to achieve it. This is called the Pygmalion effect – named after a sculptor in

Greek mythology who fell in love with a statue of his own making. Aphrodite, the goddess of love, then turned it into a real-life being.

The opposite, called the Golem effect, happens when low expectations, say from managers, teachers or parents leads us to indulge in self-harming behaviour further leading to failure, as expected of us. A doctor's pessimistic diagnosis and behaviour can lead to severe consequences for his patients. This is probably the reason why doctors are generally optimistic and some faith healers even resort to placebos, to keep up a person's spirit.

The other prominent effect seen in our day-to-day life, is the Halo effect. It basically means the positive impression that a person, brand or company makes in one area influences us in expecting a positive effect in other areas too. For example, employers rate the performance of some employees more highly than others based on their overall positive impression of them, may be biased due to being well-groomed or well-spoken rather than actual performance. The term Halo has in fact been used as an analogy to the halo drawn around saints in paintings, to create a lofty impression on people and bias their judgment.

Advertising firms use this to their advantage when they use the "halo" of movie stars, sports persons and other high achievers in one area to associate them with a brand and increase sales. We do not pause to think whether the star asking us to buy a car brand actually knows about it or should we rather listen to our local mechanic who services the cars regularly. In fact, the automobile industry regularly uses limited edition top end luxury models called "Halo cars", like an Audi R8, to draw in people to buy low end models.

However, expectations are not always synonymous with positive things. Think of a salesman being able to sell more by taking advantage of our bias towards him for being handsome or well dressed. Would you rather prefer to be treated by a competent doctor or a handsome one?

The reverse called the Horn or devil effect happens when a person's negative characteristic in one area creates bias in other areas too. How often have we judged a person's ability to perform based on looks or other unrelated characteristics?

The key may be to find a balance between reasonable and unreasonable expectations. To expect an artistically gifted but mathematically average student to get into an IIT is setting him up for failure. Would it not be better to have a conversation, consider their preference, find a reasonable target and then set expectations, so they can aspire for and achieve it? Unrealistic or rigid expectations can lead to a sense of failure, depression and in some cases suicide. The world is full of opportunities and a few lost ones do not define the rest of our lives.

Expectations are premeditated resentments too. We expect people to behave in a certain way but when they do not, we end up resenting them. It may be due to a mismatched or unspoken expectation. You may expect a person to be nice to you but if they just do their job efficiently, should that not be enough? When we expect things from others, without their consent, it is unrealistic and can lead to disappointment and resentment. Maybe next time we should agree with our better half about who will make tea and when, rather than expecting a cup and cribbing when not getting it.

Buddha was said to have asked us to harness the power of positive thinking through his teaching of 'what you have become is what you have thought'. Positive thoughts lead to positive outcomes and other religions allude to it in various forms. The belief is also sometimes called the law of attraction, defined as being able to attract things into your life through the power of positive thoughts. While movies have popularised this concept, we do need to appreciate that our expectations have to be realistic positive thoughts with a follow up plan to achieve it, rather than random wishes.

If we temper our expectations with a measure of reasonable and optimistic outlook, we will be able to welcome happiness into our lives. We will be grateful to God for what we receive and avoid disappointments.

Meanwhile, I wonder when my cousin is sixty years old will he look back at his gap year with fond memories or will he look back at it as a gap in his memories he missed filling out, by trying to measure up to his parents' expectations? I hope, for his sake, he makes the right choice.

Progress is impossible without change, and those who cannot change their minds cannot change anything.

— George Bernard Shaw

8. OTT: Revolutionising the Entertainment Industry

Last evening, we had a movie night. I got popcorn, a sweet flavour for me, and settled down with my friends to watch a new movie. The difference, we were all in our own homes, watching in sync on the OTT platform Netflix, while chatting over a video call.

The pandemic is changing our entire way of our life. The fundamental definition of every word and activity has changed. As with other things, this new movie experience has been the case over the last few months now.

By the time life returns to normal, this may well become the new normal, as we may no longer wish to risk stepping into the confines of a theatre. Instead we are looking at recreating alternative entertainment experiences like watching over OTT, from the comfort of our homes. The entire theatre experience may become a luxury rather than the norm and many of us may do it occasionally rather than regularly.

OTT, acronym for Over the Top, is the streaming of entertainment and media, using the internet. Basically, there are three OTT revenue models; AVOD (free and ad-supported services like Roku), TVOD (transactional services such as iTunes, Vimeo On Demand and Amazon Rent or buy Video that allow users to pay for individual pieces of content) and the most prevalent model SVOD (subscription-based services such as Netflix, Amazon Prime, Apple TV+, Disney+ etc). Of course, companies like Amazon have hybrid models of SVOD & TVOD, where you can watch some content free, as part of the subscription and buy or rent others.

According to PwC's Global Entertainment & Media Outlook 2019–2023, India's OTT video market will grow at a 21.8 per cent Compound annual growth rate from INR 4464 crores in 2018 to Rs. 11976 crores in 2023. This was released in June so are pre-Covid estimates and may have been nudged further up now.

The OTT model originally gained traction among the tech savvy millennials. However, with the growth of smart phone usage and faster internet it then found purchase across generations. Now the confinement has led to a massive growth in OTT over the first quarter. Netflix singlehandedly added 16 million new subscribers in the first quarter of 2020, more than double of the Wall Street prediction.

The primary attraction of OTT is its ability to offer a wide variety of content, personalised for individual users, sometimes in the same family. While children in Gen Alpha may opt for cartoons and superhero themed movies, we can have old hits, romantics and all types of movies catering to everyone's preference, in addition to releasing the latest movies online.

In fact OTT platforms leverage the use of Data Analytics and Artificial Intelligence to evaluate consumption and personalise content for every individual profile, even within one account. This analysis ultimately feeds into fine tuning the production of movies and TV shows itself.

It not only helps earn money for old movies and TV shows that were once popular but even new movies can be released via OTT assuring them a guaranteed return. Post pandemic, when theatres open, they can also have a second release via OTT after an initial theatre release. If people wait, they can watch it later at a fraction of the cost of the theatre experience and by spending much less time.

Even buying the latest movies to watch on the release day, via TVOD services, cost way less than taking the whole family out considering transport, ticket and food costs. In addition to this, the comfort of not needing to sync everyone's calendar, being able to watch it multiple times and to pause and play just adds to the allure, in our time constrained lives.

On another front, it will also help decrease and eradicate piracy over time, as the market itself will cease to exist, with everything being legally available at some point.

Theatres see it as a threat right now. Most of us are aware of the controversy surrounding the scathing official statement released by INOX, condemning production houses' decision to release their movies via OTT and skipping the indefinite uncertainty of the theatrical release. It will probably be taught in B-Schools as a case study of how not to write corporate communication. Although INOX learnt a lesson and PVR did a commendable job of it, the fear of losing control was palpable from the two largest cinema chains.

However, given the situation, the way forward may not be a case of either theatre or OTT but a case of complimenting each other.

The concept of Friday releases, date clashes and number of shows may become irrelevant, when you can release a movie every day of the week at a much lower cost to a much larger audience.

OTT opens up new markets as the audience base will increase overtime. There will be no seat restriction on the number of people and number of times they watch, so overall the market dynamics will change. It may result in expansion of the industry with new jobs and opportunities on both sides of the proverbial scene.

It may even level the playing field for people who do not have clout but have talent, as the power to choose will shift back to the audience. The audience can decide which movie and who to watch, rather than be forced to watch a handful of carefully curated movies and released on a particular day, by the powerful media houses.

It may also result in the box office success rules being redefined, as we can no longer depend on the theatre earnings of the first day or first week to measure success.

The OTT platform itself has to evolve over time. Netflix could not rest on its laurels despite a bumper Q1 as its shares fell after earnings missed in Q2 due to weak subscriber guidance for the third quarter of 2020. The reason it gave was most users had already subscribed in Q1.

Adding the complexity of data security due to content personalisation and impending market regulation, the OTT platforms themselves face many challenges to find growth in a market that is going to get increasingly competitive.

It will be interesting to watch how the entire entertainment and media industry reacts to this seismic shift and where it moves, in the next few years.

Meanwhile, the audience will grow both in terms of size and in terms of their demands. It may result in additional quality content tailored to our preferences, being available for our consumption, across multiple platforms.

We, the audience, may turn out to be the ultimate winners in this entertainment revolution.

❖❖❖

For me the core principles of privacy online are transparency, choice and control.

— Marissa Mayer

9. Shall I Invite Google, Alexa or Siri Over To My House?

I was intrigued when I was told Spotify is offering its premium customers a Google Nest Mini, for free, in September 2020. Of course, it was in some selected countries with the usual fine print of the offer being valid till the end of September or till stocks last. While I was still thinking over whether I should take the plunge and finally invite either Google or Alexa into my house, the rest of the world had ordered and the offer closed in under four days due to stocks being over.

It was the second such offer I had recently encountered and one of the many being thrown around to entice users, all over the world. The monetary value of the Google Nest mini or Amazon echo dot individually are not much and they are being heavily discounted or actually given away for free, as part of a partner deal. With their ease of use they are being touted as the latest gadget to have in our house and clearly, given the response, it is picking up in popularity.

However, if large technology companies are so keen to have their equipment in our house that they are willing to give them for free, maybe we should be asking the question why rather than jumping at the first opportunity. After all they are not here to do charity and incur loss but are sure to recoup it in some way.

On the surface of it, it seems simple enough. People are slowly moving away from web browser based searches to voice searches. Google and Amazon are the largest players in the market and they are keen on having their product readily available to fulfil this need.

Then there is the profit from our loyalty to their product environment. Let us assume we order an Amazon echo dot speaker and Alexa comes into our house. She will make our life comfortable, become part of our family and fade into the background. When we order stuff for shopping, by default it will order from Amazon store. No more Google as the middleman to compare and shop and then maybe reach it. Amazon music becomes our default playlist and Amazon algorithms now control our future shopping, news and music suggestions. If we opt for Google, well then, they will harvest our data and push us into their brand of music and services. It is pure and simple business.

You may say, so what? Well, the issues do not stop there, do they? In this instance there is a heftier cost in terms of our data, our privacy and our mental malleability. The companies survive on our data and use it to make money, through mapped products and service ads.

The most glaring issue staring at us is the security of our data and privacy rights, what with the speaker always listening in to our conversations. Security is preventing the unauthorised access to our data and privacy is about the rights we have to control the use of our personal information.

The recent incident revealed by independent researchers around the Alexa bug that let hackers install or remove apps on a device without the owners' knowledge, just by one click of a malicious link shows the security vulnerability. Sometimes the companies themselves share our data, causing breach of our privacy, albeit via our consent, courtesy the initial long T&C most of us agree to without reading.

In the past they have let their employees and third parties listen into conversations "to improve response". When it was revealed that Apple was letting third party contractors listen in, there was a backlash. Apple have since brought in an updated policy that prevents third party access while Google and Amazon have let users "opt out" of this feature. So, unless you have manually disabled it, someone, somewhere could be still listening to your fights and your sweet nothings. Would we have someone physically sit at our house and listen to everything we say, record it and share it with others randomly? Is that acceptable? If not, why should we allow it virtually?

Assuming we manage to opt out of all "human review", aka human listening by opting out of the "Help Improve Amazon Services and Develop New Features" and regularly monitor and delete your chat history, we still have to think of the influence on us by the AI algorithms. They have the power to shape our very thoughts and outlook through Artificial Intelligence algorithms.

When we ask for news, Alexa tells us what it thinks will interest us, based on analysis and Amazon's set preference and views, unless we ask specific questions. The more you choose the more data they gain and over time this means our news, music, shopping and even our cooking is being slowly driven by the choices subtly made by us and it. For example, if I search for Priyanka Chopra's latest book, it will keep showing me news about her, sometimes at the cost of other information.

I personally do not want to be typecast based on a curious search, even politically, and would much rather have the freedom to consider various options before I form my own personal view. Using Alexa or Google takes it away from me and I am an adult. Imagine the impact this has on young children, whose brains and personalities are still developing. Will it limit and channel their experience in a certain direction? One choice from them on classical music can lead to Alexa bombarding them with repeats of similar types of music However, an accidental negative word search can also lead them down a rabbit hole where they feel the whole world thinks that way. That is the power and fallacy of AI induced suggestions and it can be extremely dangerous for children.

Alexa and Google or any voice assistant for that matter have their advantages and can make life easy via voice commands. We are surrounded by tech options to help monitor our loved ones and our possessions, to help alleviate our minds of anything untoward happening to them. We just need to be cognisant of the risks, use them safely and always monitor and control our usage. However, if we let them harvest our data, influence us with their algorithms and typecast us then we make ourselves vulnerable both physically via security leaks and mentally through subtle manipulations.

While it may be fun to install and hear it recite the news over breakfast and tell us jokes or play music over dinner, is it worth the tradeoff? It may have an attractive sexy lovable voice, as agreed by a small set of men in a survey, but it is anything but attractive in repercussions, unless managed. It is a lovely device to have and interact with but remember it is a technology not a person with morals, hence needs to be controlled with appropriate settings. So, the next time you think of using or even inviting Alexa or Google over to your house, please weigh the risks versus the need and learn to actively manage your privacy before taking the plunge.

❖ ❖ ❖

There is nothing outside of yourself, look within. Everything you want is there – you are That.

– Rumi

10. A Minister for Loneliness: To Balance Physical vs Mental Health

Last weekend was Diwali. The house was filled with light, colourful decorations and plenty of food. What was missing was sound, the sound of chatter, of laughter and of children playing around. We tried to make up for the absence of friends and family through video calls and social media messages, but it still felt lonely. In fact, loneliness or a sense of emptiness seems to be a common theme that most people spoke of during my recent interactions.

In the past we used to have large joint families, with the elders caring for the children and later being cared for, in their old age. There were neighbours with roots and family ties going back generations. People used to live nearby, if not in the same towns at least in the same state. Essentially, we were surrounded by kith and kin, so we had a social support system and the chances of having meaningful interactions were higher. More importantly, we had time and an attitude to actually have those physical interactions.

In the last few decades the world has shrunk figuratively, as people moved away from tightly knit clusters to individualistic nuclear families, mostly at distant locations. Children grow up in pockets of immediate family with mostly one or sometimes no siblings at all. They see grandparents and relatives, at best annually and rarely stay with them for long. The pressures of a hectic work schedule and a struggle for existence in a competitive world takes its toll on our social life.

Although our fastpaced lifestyle is suitable for the current requirements, it also results in very few people developing roots, both for person and place. Once the children fly the nest, for studies and then for working in faraway cities or even abroad, the tightly knit unit breaks, with rarely any fall back option. It leaves parents struggling to cope with the solitude of an empty and quiet nest and the children having to start all over again, this time alone. Even retirement and lack of a busy daily schedule can initiate a feeling of loneliness, especially if there is no alternative social life.

In addition to this, while technology has driven us closer in terms of accessibility and reachability, it tends to replace actual physical interaction. Afterall texting a friend does not give us the same happiness as a hug or embrace.

All these factors, individually or combined, can lead to mental and physical loneliness. Usually it is associated with older people but in actuality, it can affect anyone, at any age. An active octogenarian with a lively friends' circle and social life could be perfectly fine, even though they may miss their family. Whereas young outgoing adults, working and living alone in a city can be lonely, if they have no real friends or meaningful interaction with the people around. Just being surrounded by people is not enough.

Loneliness is not just physical solitude, although it is a major contributing factor, but it can be a state of mind too. In fact, chronic loneliness is characterised by a feeling of being alone or isolated from people, inability to meaningfully connect or socialise, deep-rooted feelings of inadequacy, poor self-esteem, self-loathing and a reduced capacity to concentrate and take decisions.

Loneliness is one of the biggest public health challenges of recent times with evidence showing that loneliness can be just as bad as obesity or smoking. Chronic loneliness can result in an increase of the hormone Cortisol which in turn can lead to other issues like weight gain. If this persists over a period of time, it can lead to mental health issues like depression, sleeping disorders and even substance abuse. Subsequently it can lead to high blood pressure, heart diseases and can result in reducing the lifespan of people.

In the UK, a survey conducted a few years ago concluded that up to a fifth of all UK adults feel lonely most or all the time. Unsurprisingly, the numbers are similar across the world.

This has been exacerbated by the pandemic. As Covid-19 affects our physical health, we have lockdowns or restrictions which in turn impact the finances of the individual and the nation. However, it also impacts the mental health of the nation, with loneliness being a leading issue. People can go for days, weeks or even months without seeing a single soul. Even the usual banter with the postman or the shopkeepers, which meant some form of human interaction, now seem a distant dream. Most of us call or shop online with everything delivered to our doorsteps, with zero personal interaction, to minimise risk.

The important question is do we acknowledge this issue? Without acceptance of a problem, we cannot move towards a solution.

On the positive side, this can be overcome with awareness and some socially coordinated effort. If you are lonely or know someone who could be, reach out. Most people will welcome it. Try joining a regular activity like volunteering, a hobby club, walking group, etc. These will help boost your self-esteem and provide a satisfying and safe way to connect with others. They can even help elevate endorphins and serotonin levels, the happy hormones. If there is a deeper issue like substance abuse or loss of loved ones, joining or building a support group would enable in getting help and encouragement, to ease the loneliness. In case of deep-rooted issues, a mental health professional can help but this is required only for extreme cases.

In 2018, the then Prime Minister of UK, Theresa May, based on a report recommendation, created a ministerial lead for loneliness, popularly known as "Minister for Loneliness". The "strategy sets out a powerful vision for addressing this generational challenge" with steps like "incorporating loneliness into ongoing policy decisions", "embedding loneliness into relationships education classes so children in primary and secondary schools can learn about loneliness and the value of social relationships" and even accessing the impact of technology on loneliness. Some UK doctors practise "'social prescribing" which entails working with a community worker to tailor a social interaction plan for improving one's health and well-being, rather than defaulting to medicines.

Maybe nations across the world need a Minister for Loneliness too, who can look after the mental health of the population, rather than just the physical aspect. This is applicable for the current state of affairs in our society and is even more imperative during the pandemic. It is time for us to acknowledge this silent killer.

Meanwhile, if you want to check that your friend, family or even neighbour are doing well, go ring that doorbell to see for yourself. Don't just go by what they message you, tell you or when they smile for you while looking at the camera on their phone. The physical reality can be different from the virtual pretensions and an actual hug can work wonders. If you can't meet them during this pandemic, then request a friend or neighbour to drop in for a cup of tea, if required maintaining the two meters distance, so they can get some company and you can have peace of mind.

We may not have a Minister for Loneliness yet, but loneliness is a reality many people live with. If we can help to alleviate it, even partially, it is worth our while.

❖❖❖

Our society is much more interested in information than wonder, in noise rather than silence. And I feel that we need a lot more wonder and a lot more silence in our lives.

– Fred Rogers

11. Zoom Fatigue:
A Case Against Excessive Video Calls

It is early evening and as I wrap up my last meeting for the day, close the laptop and go in search of a cup of tea, my phone starts ringing. It is a close friend calling for a chat. My face lights up on seeing her name but then I feel frustrated, as it is a video call and I really could do with a break. I cancel the call, put on my earphones and dial her back for a long relaxing voice chat, while enjoying my tea.

Later I wonder, am I the only one feeling like me and my house is always on display. A quick google search tells me excessive video calls is causing a phenomenon called "Zoom fatigue", a mental fatigue caused by overloading our senses.

In today's world of WhatsApp, Facetime, Skype, Hangout and Zoom, among various others, I may be in the minority. My Mother keeps complaining that I "never" appear on video when others' children, the forever benchmark of ideal behaviour whose identities always remain shrouded in mystery, do.

I agree that having easy access to video calling is a blessing. With families spread across the thousands of kilometres, it is possibly the only way to actually see each other frequently. Happy moments of being able to see your grandchild for the first time, born across continents, is priceless. It enables us to pay our last respects to a loved one, even more pertinent in the Covid-19 world, where travel is near impossible.

However, excessive video calls are not good for your mental health. There are actually two facets to the problem. The first is about overloading our mental processes, especially in group calls and second is the visual itself and what it conveys.

In a voice call we focus on the one aspect, the voice. It means we work better at shutting down other factors, resulting in a better quality of conversation. While in a video call, we have to work hard to decode the multiple aspects of facial expression, pitch and tone of voice, body language and even reading the reactions of a screen full of faces. While this comes naturally to us in-person, almost as a background process, in a video call our brain works hard to do it consciously. This often leads to lost focus on the actual conversation and mental fatigue, over time.

It makes the whole call not only ineffective but often counterproductive to the very reason for having it, which was effective communications with the ability to read expressions.

In a personal context we are unable to manage the dynamics between family or friends, as we are unable to tune into their inherent reactions. Imagine your mother speaking about meeting a friend but you cannot keep track of your sister's expression changing, as your attention is focused on your mother's face only. Who knows what you missed or what it may escalate to later on?

The next issue is the visual itself and what it conveys. I am not talking about just your personal look, although no one likes being viewed in pyjamas with frizzy hair, but of the whole background in view. Just like a picture says a thousand words, your background tells a lot about you. It is like inviting everyone home and sharing about yourself. It is an invasion of privacy.

This becomes even more apparent in workplace or educational institutions, which have traditionally been great equalisers, being a place where only you and your capability matter. However, a video call lets people see and sometime judge, based on others social and economic aspects. Think of a bright but financially challenged student trying to fit in at school. We effectively lose the level playing field.

While some video services let us mask or conceal our backgrounds, they generally need high spec hardware and this brings out the financial disparities even further.

Then there is the case of inquisitive people folks trying to assess your personal life or possessions. Everyone has a distant cousin who wants to see the view from your window when mostly they want to see the size of your house or garden.

Sometimes it is not always about hiding but displaying too. Some people make it a point to have their perfect house, perfect family, etc., on full display.

On the one hand, it is heartening to see a friendly face after a long time or share a lovely view and a photograph does not always cut it. Sometimes it's can be a life saver in case of an emergency too. On the other, an overdose of anything is bad.

The move towards it being expected as a social etiquette makes it stressful. It should always be an option and not a social compulsion.

Exactly like I try to keep my personal details away from social media, I do not want them on full display in a video call too. Neither do I want to take stress about how I or my house looks. So, for now, I will work towards keeping them to essential video calls only.

Meanwhile, to keep my mother happy, I do a short video call to ensure she is well, let her see me along with the jasmine she planted doing well, then switch to audio for a more meaningful conversation.

❖❖❖

Nothing eases suffering like human touch.
— Bobby Fischer, Chess Meets of the Century

12. The Human Touch:
Will the Next Generation Shun It?

The other day I went to the park for a walk, of course keeping my two metres distance, due to Covid-19 restrictions. It was heartening to see a handful of people exercising and a few families even playing games. A diverse and thankfully dispersed crowd, trying to go about their life on a warm and sunny afternoon, all while following the "rules".

Suddenly, out of nowhere, a charming toddler came running up to me on her unsteady legs, hands outstretched, smiling like an angel. Maybe, like me she too seemed pleased to see people and wished to interact with them. I however, unlike my normal self, tried to cover my panic with a fake smile and frantically looked for her parents/guardian to stop her. Given the new social distancing norms my pre-conditioned human reaction of smiling back and interacting with her was useless. They were fortunately nearby and cried out for her to stop and go back to them, anxiety laced in their voice.

Her smile faded, as the child tottered back to them. The joy left my heart too and as I continued my walk, I ruminated what effect this type of interaction will have on her and on countless other childrens like her.

They are the voiceless generation, the younger they are the quieter their voice. In typical human form, they will soak up the situation and learn to adapt to the environment around them.

Yes, they will thrive under any condition but the important question is will they know any different? It is exactly this characteristic that may make them one of the worst affected by this Covid-19 pandemic, unacknowledged.

Covid-19 ground the world to a halt, both physically and metaphorically in 2020. Governments around the world, having rightly prioritised the physical well-being of its citizens and based on their capacity to care for them, brought in social distancing measures in place.

The economic impact of the widespread lockdown has been well documented with the number of articles and conversations in print and social media being limitless. The mental well-being of adults has also been spoken about in pockets. This is all encouraging news for adults. However, do we acknowledge, leave aside plan for managing, the mental impact of social isolation on our next generation, our "younglings" in Jedi speak.

We all agree that the current situation will not change much in the near future. We will have to maintain social distance till we find a vaccine and may be even later. The conversations with strangers sitting next to us while travelling look distant and Pyrex glass separates us in restaurants and even in supermarket tills.

Meanwhile what are the children being conditioned to act like? They are being asked to speak virtually and refrain from any physical contact outside their immediate family. Like the little angel I met, will they not hear the fear in their parents' voice when they move close to another human and imbibe the implication?

We now see this in the slightly older children, who seem happy to interact with their friends virtually and do not seem to miss the physical connection at all. They not only study and play together online, but also do movie nights together by watching entertainment and interacting over video calls. They have adapted and do not want to meet anyone physically, as it is too much hard work apparently. As parents, we seem delighted to see them cope, but have we thought of the long-term impact?

On a sliding scale of the need to meet people physically and age, it is directly proportional with a sharp decrease in physical interaction as age decreases. This begs the question how much will the pandemic hasten or accelerate this process? Going forward will this turn to zero with people seeking no physical interaction at all?

Touch signals safety and trust. Adults miss and cry for a hug or embrace now, while waiting for it to happen. Will the children learn to suppress the natural desire to touch and condition themselves to avoid it altogether? Does this not have a long-term impact on the way humanity will behave post-2020?

There is a high probability that the next generations will see a dramatic decrease in physical proximity. The social norms on being tactile may change permanently. Should this not be studied urgently? Can we plan for it as part of the social distancing or physical distancing measures, as a few of us prefer to call it?

Perhaps our children will shun all human contact in the near future and we will condone it, given the circumstances.

The worry about whether to greet with a hug, a handshake or a namaste may be the least of our concerns, when the next generation refuses all forms of touch itself.

❖❖❖

The best thing about a picture is that it never changes, even when the people in it do.

– Andy Warhol

13. Are We Airbrushing away Reality?

A photograph says a thousand words. Its aim is to record, to capture a true representation of the world around us. One photo can convey the emotion and the drama far better than a long description. After all, most of us do not have the ability of Shakespeare or Jane Austen.

The word photography has a Greek origin, essentially meaning "drawing with light". Photographers will tell you all about the importance of light and how capturing it just right helps create so many variations of the same image.

While ancient photography through use of camera obscura existed as early as the 4th century, modern photography can be traced back to the 17th century. We have come a long way from a single photoetching taking hours to the world of instant photography. Today most people have the ability to take an instant digital picture using their smartphones and freeze their memories for at least the foreseeable future, if not eternity, due to risk of data loss.

Photographs have the power to evoke deep emotions in us, be able to influence us by elucidating authenticity through the power of imagery. A photo is supposed to represent reality, as is.

But what if the photograph is a lie, a falsehood? What if the photo projects an artificial unreal image?

Today we are surrounded by digitally manipulated pictures on social media, magazines, websites and in advertisements, promoting airbrushed people with no signs of aging and with altered body shapes, to give the person a flawless skin with a tiny waist or similar impossible figures.

It could be through the use of Instagram filters for enhancing the image, photoshopping and airbrushing but today, establishments and public figures, more often than not, distort reality and present an alternate non-existent version to the public.

Basic photoshops are frequently done by celebrities and Instagram influencers who depend on the right "image" for popularity. It can be harmless like positioning themselves in places or with people they have never seen, to influence their followers and peddle a lie. The more serious form of doctoring is around digitally distorting face and body shapes of people to present an unrealistic or conformist image.

It could be the *Grazia magazine* airbrushing away the curly hair of Lupita Nyong'o to make her conform to the Eurocentric social standards of beauty, that too without her permission or photoshopped celebrities flaunting a flat stomach a few days after giving birth to a baby. It could be the airbrushing away of wrinkles, changing facial features or creating thin bodies and lighter skin tones of models and actors, making them look younger instead of older, as they age. It could be skinny models made to look healthy or vice versa, whatever the situation demands.

Although more effected, it is not limited to women. Images of men are also altered to remove wrinkles, give a squared jaw and add muscles. When stars like Justin Beiber in Calvin Klein or Matthew McConaughey in Dolce & Gabanna advertisements could not escape being enhanced to apparently look "better", what can be said for the rest of us?

Reality stars like Kim Kardashian and Instagram influencers are epic examples of people using photoshop to paint a rosy picture of everything, to make money from it. They send out a misleading message about unattainable beauty standards for the general public. We subconsciously desire to imitate and feel dejected when we fail to achieve it.

Some fashion and cosmetic brands market their products with heavily edited images, to showcase a supposedly achievable perfect result after using them. People buy it, assuming they will attain similar effects. When they are unable to realise the exaggerated and morphed outcomes, it propagates negative thoughts of inadequacy, especially among susceptible youngsters. Ultimately it plays into our own insecurities about body image and social standards of beauty.

The Instagram generation frequently photoshop and fix "flaws" before posting images on social media. Meanwhile the older generation are fixated on having an even skin tone and hide dark circles all while trying to look young. With a multitude of apps available this is fairly easy to achieve, even on a phone. People often feel the pressure to conform to an unrealistic and increasingly high expectations of beauty and it can lead to low self-esteem and even eating disorders.

Interestingly and infrequently, photos are altered to convey negativity. *Time magazine* published a doctored version of a photograph of O.J. Simpson on its cover in the early 1990s, making him look darker and more menacing to manipulate people's perspective, during the ongoing trial. It is an early version of using a filter, making this an old phenomenon which has become more prevalent now, due to growth in social media. Sometimes people doctor images to showcase a fake image with malicious intent causing harm to others on purpose. Once the image is available online, it is very difficult to convince people that it is fake.

However, many celebrities from the entertainment industry are speaking up against the trend of presenting an alternate reality. Their effort to present an authentic image of themselves along with the social movement towards acceptance of all body shapes being beautiful or acceptable is bringing in a ray of hope. UK-based make-up artist and model Sasha Pallari has recently launched the hashtag #filterdrop campaign to promote confidence in real beauty, rather than the artificially enhanced version using Instagram filters.

Instagram itself acknowledges the issue to some extent and is working on limiting the effect of this augmented reality. However, it is neither the only one responsible nor will it damage its own popularity by tampering with the very social structure on which it has built its success.

The onus is on us to realise that our "flaws" are good and they make us who we are. They are proof of a life well lived. They capture a true picture, just like a photo is meant to, so we can have authentic memories, rather than unrealistic ones. I hope no one would want to look back at a picture of their digitally altered baby but would rather want an authentic memory. Then why do it to yourself?

We need to appreciate that creating an impossible image is all about glamorising a product or a person to make it aspirational. Creating fantasy is part of selling a product, be it a consumable like say makeup, a person like a movie star or even the medium like a magazine or a movie. We as consumers need to be able to differentiate between fantasy and glamour from reality, to be able to view it objectively.

Perhaps it is time we have a law that airbrushed pictures should come with a tag or a fine print of what has been changed, so we know what is real and what is not. Then we can make an informed choice to go about imitating them in real life or making mental adjustments to the perceived reality.

❖❖❖

True happiness is not attained through self-gratification, but through fidelity to a worthy purpose.

— *Helen Keller*

14. Is it Time to Trade Happiness for Purpose?

In the initial months of lockdown, I spent a lot of time watching exciting TV series and movies as a means of escaping from the boredom and stagnation surrounding us. However, as the months progressed every time I watched something exciting it left me feeling sad rather than happy. Was it just my mind comparing the fast paced happening life on screen with the slow and uncertain life surrounding me or seeking transient happiness through traditional methods was yielding fewer results? I am not alone as there seems to be a universal feeling of increasing levels of unhappiness around us.

Human beings need both physical and mental health to live a fulfilling life. While working towards physical health is quite self-explanatory, attaining mental health through a balanced mind is a challenge in the best of times, so is proving to be even more complex in the current unprecedented situation.

Traditionally we have looked at happiness as the key to achieving our mental well-being. Our entire social construct is based on hedonism. It is expected that everyone will seek happiness be it in terms of name, fame, money and relationships. All those breaking ranks are seen as detractors, as aberrations to the norm.

Happiness is usually defined as an emotional state of being in a positive mood ranging from contentment to joy. However, does seeking happiness make us mentally balanced and give us lasting satisfaction? Countless research and almost all religious teachings state to the contrary.

If you ask a homeless man, he would probably say basic necessities like food, clothing and shelter would make him happy. Yet, are people with the basic necessities truly happy?

They probably want something more and this turns into a never-ending quest.

The standard of living across the world has improved over the centuries. Life as we know it has become much safer, comfortable and filled with opportunities for the general public, yet the level of happiness has nosedived rather than risen.

So how do we find mental balance and contentment? We can have a lasting sense of gratification by pursuing meaning and purpose, rather than chasing the transient feeling of being happy. Research has shown that people who live life with a purpose are much more resilient and have higher levels of mental peace than those without.

Purpose is about working towards a goal, contributing towards others' happiness and well-being, rather than just our own. A doctor's purpose is to save lives. If you ask teachers, they would probably be proud of the achievements of their students rather than their designation or actual job.

This is even more relevant in the current situation. The pandemic and subsequent restrictions make us feel unhappy and isolated. We feel a loss in purpose as we are unable to continue with our regular life, from which we generally derived satisfaction. It has led to increased levels of anxiety and mental stress, may be due to changes in physical, familial or financial circumstances.

Often we hear people complain about being worried about the future or fed up with the current state and feel restless with life itself. Elderly people, especially those not busy with office and young children, feel a sense of hopelessness from being away from family and friends or their usual social activities, which used to be their lifeline. These negative thoughts can in some cases even lead to a mild or severe depression.

We can overcome this by finding some meaning and purpose in life. It does not have to be a lofty charitable goal but a simple project using your strengths or based on your hobby or pastime could help.

Everyone can find some way of contributing towards the well-being of our society and gradually develop it into a long-term purpose in their life. Let us say you can sew, why not help sew masks and donate them to key workers? If you cannot sew but are actually good at organising, maybe you can help organise donations or orchestrate this event in your community. If you love reading you can provide online book reviews or record audiobooks. Even supporting children learning from home, especially with parents who struggle to help them, would be constructive.

You do not need any special skills or education for attaining purpose in life. All you need is a desire to do something meaningful, to explore your interests and available opportunities, then work towards something that provides the elusive feeling of contentment.

The pandemic is finally giving us the opportunity to slow down, step back and reappraise at our single-minded pursuit of socially acceptable ways of seeking happiness. It is giving us an opportunity to redefine our lives, to recognise things that truly matter to us and find a goal for contributing towards our society and consequently our own well-being.

Acting on it may help give us lasting fulfilment and bring a sense of value to our lives. It may keep us motivated and start our day with a determination to achieve something, rather than face another day of oblivion.

❖❖❖

If you're trying to persuade people to do something, or buy something, it seems to me you should use their language, the language in which they think.

— David Ogilvy

15. Inclusive Marketing:
Reflecting or Driving Social Change

Today's consumers are knowledgeable, tech savvy and demanding. They prefer to consume brands which showcase an authentic reflection of the world around them along with a core alignment with their values. They want to use products which they can relate to, be it fast moving consumer goods, tech, entertainment or even major purchases like cars and holidays.

Previously companies relied on aspirational marketing strategies to promote an ideal standard for a specific target group. For example, food and cooking products were targeted towards women, shown as living in a beautiful house with perfect families. However, social changes have started to unravel the stereotypes. Most women work, men cook and single parents can be just as happy. The clearly defined stereotypes have gone for a toss, especially among the GenX & GenY, who account for all consumers under forty years old.

Add to this mix, the rise in consciousness around equality and discrimination, now people have started questioning the very paradigms of social behaviour. So, companies try catering to the changing attitudes by bringing in diversity and inclusivity in their ads through inclusive marketing.

In short, inclusive marketing is marketing that showcases important factors like age, ethnicity, income, class, sexuality, language and religion, amongst others. It aims to communicate and connect with a larger cross section of the audience by providing a reflection of them.

Inclusive marketing starts with having an inclusive product. A makeup range only meant for fair skin tones is inherently biased and needs to be redesigned. Pop icon Rihanna's Fenty beauty makeup line, catering to a diverse range of skin tone got it right both at the product and marketing levels and keeps selling out in record numbers. A fierce backlash from consumers for promoting colourism forced Hindustan Unilever Limited to change its product "Fair & Lovely" to "Glow & Lovely".

Another example of product alignment could be Mattel Inc. realising their unrealistically narrow-waisted blonde Barbies were outdated and not being bought by customers, as they neither identified nor connected with them. So, they revamped their dolls to reflect social diversity. Since then they have included dolls of all skin tones and body shapes, resulting in a phenomenal increase in sales. Their top sellers last year were a curvy black doll with an afro and one in a wheelchair.

Next, the product needs to speak to a diverse crowd. A car can be bought and driven by a man or a woman, young or old, family or bachelor, so having representation across the board would help reach a wider audience base. Research shows that almost 70 to 80 per cent of purchasing decisions are made by women, yet ads primarily target men. Inclusive marketing around gender may help make products more relatable and increase their brand identity and sale.

The best way to make a product relatable is to showcase people using them is real life situations. However, the user base is wide and combined with the need to adhere to capricious socially acceptable norms, the marketing teams have their work cut out.

A well intentioned marketing campaign can sometimes go terribly wrong. After all, in this age of social media and consumer power with swift repercussions, a well-received ad has the potential to bring in a lot of revenue, but one wrong move can lead to loss in millions, if not billions, for most companies.

A case in point could be the epic failure of the Dove "before and after" advert showing an African-American woman turning into a white one, implying dark skin is dirty.

The best way to avoid such pitfalls would be to have a diverse representation in the team at every stage from design to marketing it. Imagine, a team of men working on a menstrual product. Expecting them to understand the product, even with deep immersion, if that is even possible, would be difficult.

However, any publicity can be good publicity. Benetton Group, famous for its controversial ads, created the Unhate Campaign in 2011 which showed world political and religious leaders like Barack Obama and Chinese leader Hu Jintao kissing. It led to a fierce backlash. Benetton never apologised, its sales did not suffer and in fact the ad went on to win the Cannes ad film festival award.

Brands do not always reflect society but can lead social change too. By including women be it female sports persons, scientists or even a background full of people from both gender and various age groups working together, brands can help normalise situations and bring in a silent social revolution. Tata Tea usually makes socially relevant advertisements and are worth watching. P&G's Ariel advertisement addressing gender inequality by speaking about mothers teaching their sons the same things as their daughters and helping fix it from the core, was laudable.

Ads can help bring focus on typically marginalised or underrepresented voices into the mainstream and initiate progressive social change. A Microsoft ad showing real life stories of disabled children playing on adaptive Xbox controllers was a big step in this direction.

The 11-year-old Duchess Megan Markel saw a soap ad calling out "all women in America are fighting greasy pots and pans" and famously wrote letters to Procter & Gamble, as well as others like Hillary Clinton (who was the First Lady at the time) saying, "I don't think it's right for children to grow up thinking these things, that mother does everything." She tried to call attention to the influence ads have on children.

Companies need to think carefully about what they want to say and to whom. An inclusive product and marketing campaign for a diverse audience can help make the message more refined and broaden the reach, thus making it successful.

Inclusive marketing genuinely helps diverse voices be seen and heard, consequently helps in alleviating social and cultural bias. It can provide stimuli for a positive social change by creating thoughtful and respectful content, while also building a socially relevant and successful brand. When used responsibly, it can both reflect social change and help drive social change too.

Unlike a drop of water which loses its identity when it joins the ocean, man does not lose his being in the society in which he lives. Man's life is independent. He is born not for the development of the society alone, but for the development of his self.

— B. R. Ambedkar

16. Defining our Identity:
A Necessity in these Troubled Times

Who are you? Almost all of us have been asked this question in some form or other, at many points in our lives. We probably defaulted to our name, maybe a designation if it was at the workplace or identified with a relationship like a parent, child or spouse. How we responded, probably depended on the context of the person posing it.

But what exactly is our identity? It is who we are as a sum total of all the above plus a few other things. It is our qualities, our beliefs and our entire personality that make us a unique individual. Identity is who we were in the past, what we are in the present and how we and to an extent others', envisage us in the future.

The psychologist Erik Erickson proposed a framework comprising three main components, the ego or "I", our unique personal habits of "me" and the social and cultural identity of "us". Our identity or personality is a dynamic construct, a balance between these three components.

The "I" starts developing early as we grow from a baby and become increasingly aware of ourselves. The "me" develops when we are exposed to various social factors and influenced by people in our environment, from our childhood. The socio-cultural identity starts forming primarily around adolescent years, based on the social environment we grow up in. However, the "me" and the socio-cultural aspect of "us", keeps evolving throughout our lives.

The finding of ourselves in a social context is also the hardest, as we struggle to strike a balance between staying true to ourselves within the social construct available to us. Becoming too independent may lead to social alienation and make us misfits. However, conforming too much to current established social norms can lead to internal conflicts and unhappiness. Sometimes it is necessary to take a stand for our principles and our sanity.

No one is born with inherent social or religious beliefs. As we are exposed to varied perspectives, we choose what we think is right and keep developing our views. Exposure to different concepts opens up our world to diverse opinions and options. It can happen through information gathered from travel, reading, a strong personal experience, teachings, a social event or even self-realisation. Thus, something we thought was the ultimate truth in our teens may be more of a grey area in our thirties.

The internet and resulting globalisation have had a pronounced effect on this fluidity. Emigration and the subsequent biculturalism is an example. Biculturalism is when a person has exposure to two cultures and tries to fit in and identify with both. They amalgamate cultural values, pick what is comfortable, acceptable and create a unique personalised blend. Take an example of a first generation Indian American, who upholds the traditional family values of old but also does not shy away from confronting interpersonal disagreements directly, if required. They may seem opposing ideas, but most people manage to strike a balance. It helps them identify with both cultures and thrive. Their ideologies are unique and can change over time as they imbibe more values from both societies.

American academic Deborrah E. S. Frable in her research said, identity is the individual's psychological relationship to particular social category systems. She suggests that gender, racial, ethnical, sexual and class identities are fluid, multidimensional, personalised social constructions that reflect the individual's current context and socio-historical cohort.

What we are, our genetic makeup, does not change. However, who we are, can change with time, based on our social environment and with the right impetus. The whole paradigm of change of heart and reformation is based on the concept that we can change a part of our personality.

Usually society places the burden of having a well-defined strong identity on a man rather than a woman. Women are given a degree of flexibility in either having a strong identity of their own or just depend on relationships to define themselves.

However, sometimes they may be forced into a socially conformist personality driven by indoctrinated beliefs. It does not take away their identity per se, rather takes away their choice. Some culturally progressive societies advise women not to define themselves by negative, self-limiting notions like their looks, people's opinion, financial status or even their past. In any case, it is essential for everyone to have an independent identity, to be able to participate in society and live a fulfilling life.

But what if we are denied one completely? Afghan women are fighting for the right to reveal their own names. They have no named birth certificate, no name on a wedding invitation and no name even on their tombstone. They do not exist in the legal system as they have no form of ID card. No one outside their immediate family is allowed to call them by their names and they are always referred to by a relationship, as a daughter, wife, mother etc. In fact, it is considered dishonourable to even refer to a woman, outside their immediate family, by a name.

It is an extreme case of curbing the very existence of a person by denying her a legal entity, a basic human right. Here a name is an amalgamation, a representation of a personality, so denying them one is equal to stripping away their identity and making them ghosts.

Just as in the past, women were not allowed to study, vote or hold jobs in various countries and have changed now, I hope Afghan women can start their journey to create their own identities by winning this battle soon.[2]

Today we take our right to a birth certificate and other legal documents for granted and sometimes even complain when we have to create or update one. It is a privilege we should appreciate more.

We are indeed fortunate to live in a relatively modern society, which lets us develop into an independent person, with our own opinions and beliefs. It allows us to make our own decisions rather than forces us into a predetermined mould. If we stay true to our own self and our beliefs, rather than be swayed by social demands, we will live a happy and rewarding life.

Perhaps it is time we think carefully and consciously about who we are, what we stand for, what we want to do and where we want to go next. So, the next time someone questions our identity or tries to influence ours, we are better prepared to face it.

---

2   Since this article was written Afghan women have won the right to being named in legal documents.

A diverse mix of voices leads to better discussions, decisions, and outcomes for everyone.

– Sundar Pichai.

17. Business Without Bias –
A Key Mantra for Survival in Today's World

In light of recent global events and the subsequent fallout, primary amongst them being #metoo & #blacklivesmatter movements, Diversity & Inclusion or D&I for short, has become a key mantra across the world. Contributing towards this has been an increased awareness owing to ease of access to information via the extensive reach of mobile phones and social media platforms.

Between Gen Y and Gen Z, anyone under forty is covered and is the primary target, both as a workforce and as a consumer base. These generations are not only tech savvy but are very woke. They would trade their beliefs over their pay cheque any day and they are more likely to work for or buy from a brand that aligns with their values than otherwise. If anyone is found deficient they swiftly cancel them and move on.

The days of building and maintaining a macho culture for corporate success are long gone. It is not just frowned upon but if exposed can lead to a potentially existential backlash from employees, customers and shareholders. Today values like inclusivity and empathy are given brownie points and lead to long-term success.

A potential customer or employee looks up on social media and researches about the company's values, ethics and policies to gauge alignment, before they buy a product or apply for a job.

So where does this leave business? If they want to survive, they have to update their game and ensure they align their product and values with the current social thought process.

The subject of having the right value, ethos and ethics depends on a moral compass and flows down from the leadership team. It depends on how businesses conduct themselves and encompasses issues such as human rights, social responsibility, environmental and ecological stewardship along with global capitalism.

Nike took a stand when it featured Colin Kaepernick with the slogan "Believe in something. Even if it means sacrificing everything. Just Do It.", referring to his kneeling protests during the national anthem against police brutality in the US was met with heavy protests. However, Nike dug its heels in and stood by it. Although it saw a slight dip initially, overall it resulted in Nike's value increase by $6 billion, a massive positive effect by taking a stand.

However, in today's globalised and interconnected world of companies an outsider's view is not enough. A diverse workforce is needed to be able to appreciate issues, bring in authenticity, local nuances and appropriate behaviour. An example could be baby food company Gerber selling its products in Africa with a picture of a sweet baby on the bottle without realising that in Ethiopia products usually have pictures on the label of what is inside, given many consumers cannot read.

D&I can help business avoid this by celebrating the differences among people. Research has shown that companies with a diverse workforce perform better. They are able to win top talent, improve their customer and employee satisfaction, which ultimately leads to better financial returns.

It acts as a key determinant to help alleviate cultural issues, so is being spearheaded visibly by corporates now. It has become common for companies with employee friendly and D&I policies to do inclusive marketing, showcasing their ethos and creating a relatable brand, to attract customers and top talent.

The Gucci black face sweaters mishap is a perfect example of D&I failure at every level. When a model walked down the runway in Gucci 2018 Fall/Winter show wearing a turtleneck sweater resembling a blackface with red oversized lips the backlash was almost instant on social media. Gucci not only apologised and pulled out the offending item but it led to major changes in the organisation to avoid this ever happening in the future. It could be argued that if at least one black person had been part of the design team or at any stage, this could probably have never happened.

Let us be honest, we are all subject to a reality tunnel vision, wherein we have developed a subconscious set of mental filters formed from our beliefs and experiences. Thus, how we interpret the world will be different from how others see it. Having a diverse and inclusive culture leads to alternate and authentic viewpoints being brought in and helps negate the effects of reality tunnel vision.

It is relatively easy to solve diversity through updating the recruiting process to hire a diverse talent pool, representing gender, ethnic, racial, sexual orientation, age and religion amongst others.

However, having people in your organisation is not enough. Rather, engaging them at all levels through an open culture and listening to them is essential to ensure we are on the right path. Inclusion needs having an open mind, accepting and respecting people for who they are and valuing their opinions. It is a whole new work culture.

This will also help businesses balance diversity and inclusivity between groups, for taking a stance does not equate to preferring one group over another, majority or minority. The idea is to create harmony, to treat everyone as equals and not take sides.

A good principle contemplated of late is – if it is about me do not do it without me. Include people from all walks of life like race, age and gender but make sure to include people from your target audience to ensure both the product and the brand resonates with them. A product for teens should have teens in the process, if you want to reach and resonate with their thought process.

Institutionalised D&I policies, raising awareness among people about what is a conscious and unconscious bias, creating an inclusive and conducive work environment where people are free to express their opinion without repercussion and respecting everyone's views would all lead to an enriched work experience and a robust business.

It will result in attracting a diverse and engaged talent pool and have a resounding effect on having more aligned goals to the current generation. It will lead to building the right brand presence and help develop the foundation for a future in the marketplace.

Unless corporations manage to create a diverse and inclusive culture of doing business without bias and hold themselves accountable to it, it will become increasingly difficult to survive in the current world.

The way I dress depends on how I feel. I never have to psych myself up. Usually it just feels like it works.

— Rihanna

18. Comfy is the New Cool!

Last year my back muscles made their presence felt rather painfully, as a result of a minor mishap. Subsequently, I had to relook at the torture I subject them to by walking in high heels and carrying a heavy tote handbag (read imbalanced load), all day and almost every day, in the name of confirming to the dictates of fashion and portraying a sense of professionalism at work.

A chat with my physiotherapist led me to realise their negative impact and so switched to backpacks and low-heeled shoes. They made a world of difference and I felt my back thanking me for it. However, what amazed me was not my medical recovery but the world of convenience and comfort it opened up.

When I had got my first job, I had reluctantly traded my comfortable rucksack and jeans for a posh leather handbag and office wear, to create a "grownup" professional look. How have the wheels turned over the last decade? My search for office appropriate gear led me to realise that people have already begun to move back to the comfort zone.

Call it the necessity to fit in a laptop along with an environment-friendly refillable water bottle to those gym wear for an after-office workout, now one bag could get rid of a huge tote or multiple bags, while being body and travel-friendly, is a no brainer for everyone.

While there are pockets, especially in traditional financial and legal professions where conventional dress codes are still followed, the majority of workforce across the world have moved towards a more casual dressing. It is geared towards our comfort and convenience rather than complying to conventions. This means women carry backpacks to business meetings and a tie is on the verge of disappearing from the corporate realm altogether.

Meanwhile all major designers and high street brands, sensing the demand for comfortable attire and accessories, in and out of office, have already jumped on the bandwagon. With just the global handbag market being over 50 billion USD, keeping up with changing customer preference is a must, to be able to survive and thrive in the fashion industry. It is no wonder that the finest sportswear companies like Nike and Lululemon are now collaborating with fashion houses and walking down the ramp at top fashion shows.

The move away from conventional dressing to convenient dressing is a reflection of a deeper change in social attitudes and behaviour too.

The first is around the importance of taking care of oneself. Not only does your mind and body need TLC (Tender Loving Care) but wellness is considered to be the ultimate luxury. It is led by the rich and famous and followed by the rest of us. It is socially acceptable, in fact cooler, to take care of yourself and takes precedence over other social commitments or expectations. A Facebook or Instagram post of a 6 am Peloton bike ride showing your healthy body is way better than a drunk late-night snap now. So, if it means you miss going out with friends to exercise, eat healthy, go vegan or wear trendy trainers to work to prevent foot ache, it is perfectly reasonable and acceptable.

The next social change is around people expecting you to look at results instead of methods. In this context, your choice of attire does not affect your ability to work. The idea is to appear smart and presentable and to be able to perform, not dress elaborately for a performance, unless if you are actually performing somewhere. In addition to this, it is considered discriminatory to judge a person's choice of attire if it is presentable and does not impact their capability to execute the job.

Does a person wearing a suit perform better than someone in ethnic wear, just because of it? The answer is no. Then how does wearing heels over flats make any difference but it was till recently and is still frowned upon in some regressive pockets.

This feeds into the next behavioural change about people no longer caring about conforming to conventions. There is always a social pressure, through stated or unstated expectations, to look or dress a certain way but the extent of what is acceptable is far more liberal now. Women more than men, who were disproportionately impacted by social expectations, are taking it upon themselves to redefine their choice of fashion based on their individuality, need and comfort.

Leading this revolution are people at the very top of the fashion food chain, the Hollywood stars and the supermodels. It is common to see them out and about in Athleisure and others imitate. Self-made successful entrepreneur like Mark Zuckerberg, who regularly wears grey t-shirts and hoodies to office, have made an impact on our fashion choices too. They set the trend for acceptable office wear.

Pandemic and working from home have magnified this trend, making athleisure the fastest selling style. It helps us strike a balance between being presentable yet comfortable, be it in our Zoom/Hangout meetings, a trip to the supermarket or coffee with friends. Athleisure is basically casual wear that combines high-quality athleticwear with versatile leisurewear to offer comfort while maintaining style, so has the ability to be worn anytime, anywhere.

You are seen as taking a stand for your well-being and against the outdated patriarchal expectations, by going with comfort. So, comfort is definitely the new cool.

As for me, while I am not planning on donating my carefully curated but mostly impulsive bought handbag collection in the near future, I am judicious in using them based on my convenience rather than convention. A long journey, even for a work meeting, begs a backpack. Of course, the old collegiate canvas version or the hiking backpacks will not cut the mustard but a posh leather designer version matched with an appropriate attire would fit the bill. The fashion industry is bending over backwards to cater to my needs.

However, with 2020 being the year of working from home, I have packed away all my suits and designer laptop backpacks and bought some more athleisure along with a mini backpack for my occasional trip to the supermarket. After all, we still need to pack the tissues and hand sanitisers somewhere, don't we?

Technology is just a tool. In terms of getting the kids working together and motivating them, the teacher is the most important.

— *Bill Gates*

19. Deepfake: Is it the New Weapon of Choice?

Artificial Intelligence (AI) is growing by leaps and bounds and touches almost every aspect of our lives, from AI controlled autopilot planes to the spam filter in your email or the shopping suggestions on websites.

One of the main benefits of AI lies in its ability to self-train. This is being used to our advantage in developing technology like autonomous vehicles or medical diagnostics. However, this technology can be easily misused to create fear and doubt among the public, thus having far reaching effects in society. One of the top examples of such misuse is through the propagation of Deepfakes.

Deepfake is a manipulated video, created using Artificial Intelligence, so realistic that it takes an expert to be able to tell the difference. Deepfake is for videos what photoshop is for still images.

The "Deep" comes from deep learning of the AI neural networks, a type of Machine Learning (ML) technique based on the human brain. The idea is to use a GAN (Generative Adversarial Network) to train the AI. Essentially, it means two Machine Learning models are used, one creating the Deepfake and the other trying to catch it out by testing it. At some point when fake video has improved to such an extent that the other ML model cannot detect the forgery, we have a Deepfake ready to be used. It was invented in 2014 by Ian Goodfellow, a then PhD student.

In the past, the ability to create tampered videos used to be limited to a select few in the entertainment industry or by sophisticated government organisations. Deepfake took this ability and placed it in the hands of anyone who is so inclined. All they need is to download a free software app like Faceswap, a few photos of the person downloaded from social media or otherwise and in a few hours, they are able to create a Deepfake video. Of course, it does need some skill, perseverance and access to real photos/videos of the person to have a quality video but, these are freely available on social media and on the internet, especially of celebrities and politicians.

Initially, its use was limited to creating porn videos with famous faces on them or personal revenge porn. However, this has steadily progressed from targeting individuals to being used for political gains by opponents or even rogue nations as part of computational propaganda. Marco Rubio, the Republican senator from Florida and 2016 presidential candidate, dramatically called them the modern equivalent of nuclear weapons.

Politically motivated individuals, groups or even states, use it to launch a coordinated campaign, to drive a point and influence public opinion by posting disturbing videos online. The story is then spread by their thousands of associates or even artificial bots to make it viral. By the time this is verified and taken down, if ever, a small section of society has already been influenced permanently.

In today's connected world of social media, just as it is hard to suppress the truth, it is also easy to spread lies. It can help create artificial panic in the public or in the financial space. It may sway votes and even cost an election if say a video is released just before the voting day, too late to validate and call out, before casting the ballot. The US fought hard to prevent this in the November 2020 Presidential elections. Meanwhile other less developed countries or those with tighter government control are able to feed and propagate lies to their citizens, who have no means of knowing otherwise.

A fired Facebook data scientist's internal memo, published on Buzzfeed news spoke of finding "multiple blatant attempts by foreign national governments to abuse our platform on vast scales to mislead their own citizenry, and caused international news on multiple occasions. I have personally made decisions that affected national presidents without oversight and taken action to enforce against so many prominent politicians globally that I've lost count." It details how the social network knew leaders of countries around the world were using their site to manipulate voters — and failed to act, ignoring Global Political Manipulation. It illustrates the challenges facing individuals and nations, especially democracies, across the world and social media platforms themselves. The current efforts to control it are uncoordinated and a slapdash approach.

A few years ago, BuzzFeed produced a Deepfake video featuring former US President Barack Obama and comedian Jordan Peele, using After Effects CC and the FakeApp, to raise public awareness about it. Jordan, looking like President Obama, made a weird public announcement, saying: "You are entering an era in which our enemies could make it look like we're saying anything at any point in time, even if they would never say those things. So, for instance, like you can have me say things, like, I don't know... Killmonger was right." Seconds later, he appeared side by side with Obama, revealing that the video was fake.

Deepfake, per se, are a technological advancement and have multiple positive uses in industries like gaming, fashion or entertainment. It may lead us to being able to play games with our own avatars. It can also be used for dubbing in movies. David Beckham helped launch a global appeal to end malaria using a 'deepfake' malaria awareness video, where he spoke in nine languages. Will the entertainment industry reach a stage where the actors' faces are the only real thing and their bodies and voices are all fake, using Deepfake? Maybe. However, there are moral and legal downsides, like using images of actors who may have died, without their consent.

The state of California, realising the severity of impact, made them illegal but Deepfake is legal elsewhere. In the absence of official direction, many platforms are taking a stand against using them. They do not want to encourage the behaviour and would like to avoid the moral dilemma altogether.

We are attempting to regulate modern technology with ancient laws. However, any new legislation has to weigh in the benefits of this AI technology along with freedom of expression, IP rights and privacy laws. It cannot be a blanket ban. It will take time to research the advantages and implications before the law can be framed, with the technology itself and its uses still evolving.

Meanwhile, we need to be careful and critical about every video we watch, especially if it is found to be too radical or sensational. A bad Deepfake mostly has no eye blinking, wrong shadows or unnatural movements but a good one needs much more sophisticated research to detect.

It is worth checking the authenticity of the video, before believing or posting it on social media. In this world of fake news and Deepfake videos, our vigilance is the only armour we have for protection of ourselves and the society we live in.

Women are working more, men are understanding their value as caregivers, women are primary breadwinners — I mean, we could go on and on and on. Things are different. So we can't keep operating like everything is the same, and that's what many of us have done. And I think it's up to us to change the conversation.

— Michelle Obama

20. Shecession and Social Regression: An Inadvertent Impact of the Pandemic

The year 2020 turned out to be tough for everyone, be it in terms of health, wealth or just happiness. We will be hard pressed to find a person who has not been touched by the pandemic currently ravaging the world, destroying people's physical and mental health along with world economies. We are progressing towards severe recession across the world with an as yet undetermined impact, as the pandemic is still showing no signs of abating.

On the surface, it seems to be a universal phenomenon, sparing none. However, a closer inspection shows that it actually widens the existing divides, impacting the vulnerable more. For example, it is easier for white collar workers to work from home, for rich children to have access to online learning equipment and support from educated parents or for affluent people living in large houses to have the space to isolate and exercise without actually stepping out.

However, the worst impact of this discrepancy is between men and women. Women, while being statistically less impacted by the actual disease per se with respect to men, are much worse off socially and financially.

The last century has seen massive improvements in women's rights and education so subsequent employment. Yet, this has not been matched with an equal progress in terms of reduction in housework, so women used to end up working a second or double shift at home. Pre-pandemic, women performed 76.2 per cent of total hours of unpaid care work, more than three times as much as men, according to the International Labour Organisation (ILO). The pandemic has increased this proportion even more, what with the whole family being at home all the time. This has led to a "double-double shift", as coined by Facebook COO Sheryl Sandberg.

In fact, we are becoming increasingly socially regressive during the pandemic, despite the perception and plethora of WhatsApp jokes about men learning to cook and clean.

Traditionally women's jobs have been lower earning, part-time or with a degree of flexibility. They also have an inherent capability to absorb more caring responsibility. Besides, there is an expectation of the patriarchal society, where men are spared and women are trained to do housework from a young age.

Previously, at least they had maids to help. With the pandemic leading to their conspicuous absence, it has exacerbated the situation and led them to choose and cut somewhere, for their physical and mental well-being. Unsurprisingly, they choose to let go of office. It was no joke but a representation of the stress women go through, when Subarna Ghosh, started a petition to PM Modi, asking him to address the issue of men sharing housework.

It does make logical and financial sense for the women to give up paid work. After all we do need someone to stay at home and take care of the children and the elderly. Since the man mostly earns more, has a stable job, can devote more time to work and is more valued it is a no brainer what will happen. Yet, this means we are moving back to the old ways of men working outside and women doing all the household work. It means the progress we made around gender equality will regress by decades. It may be the right choice for the individual family but may not be the right choice for society.

In addition to this a larger proportion of women work in the sectors hardest hit, like leisure, travel and hospitality, education and retail sector. As these sectors are doing worse, the chances of layoff or reduction in income are inherently higher for women too. For example, a majority of the airline staff are women, so the impact will also be greater for them.

Just as in 2008, a disproportionately higher loss of blue-collared jobs led to it being termed as "mancession", the current path of recession seems to impact women more and is being widely labelled as "shecession" or a pink-collar recession.

It is a universal phenomenon, impacting women across the world. Based on actual data, the US National Women's Law Centre estimated that just in April 2020, this crisis wiped out all the job gains that women had made in the past decade.

A study of previous pandemics, like Ebola and Zika, shows that not only did women take up more care, the economic recovery was especially slow for them. This may be due to the nature of their jobs being considered less essential and the time it takes for the social demands to settle down. It also shows the deep, long-lasting effects on gender equality. While initially everyone was proportionally impacted, men bounced back rapidly but women took longer to come back to pre-epidemic levels. Sometimes it took years, as missed vaccines and preventable illnesses in children led to mothers taking time off even years later.

However, it is not all bad news. There is more acceptance and appreciation around the importance of child care and early education now, along with the contributions of women towards it. Post-pandemic investment in these sectors will result in not only more jobs but also recognition for women. It is time for us to acknowledge the unpaid efforts of women and both share and try to alleviate it.

Overall the impact of the pandemic, even though yet to be exactly quantified, is universally accepted to be severe. It is up to us at home and the government in education and employment, to ensure the impact is evenly distributed and minimise impact of this "shecession".

Technology now allows people to connect anytime, anywhere, to anyone in the world, from almost any device. This is dramatically changing the way people work, facilitating 24/7 collaboration with colleagues who are dispersed across time zones, countries, and continents.

— Michael Dell

21. Remote Working: Boon or Bane

Seamless delivery through remote working has become the new normal across the world, a win-win situation for all, given the current restrictions. The employers get to alleviate the economic effect by keeping the revenues flowing while the employees have a job, hence income, unaffected by the pandemic. This is true across a broad spectrum of non-essential white-collared services, best represented by the IT sector.

Geographically diverse teams in IT companies have always relied on this model and have implemented it in measured doses. Employees have had some flexibility in hours which allowed them to manage commitments at home like childcare, etc. The expectation was always on having the ability to be present in office, if required, at short notice. There was also an unconscious bias towards people who showed reluctance to come into office as equating to reduced productivity and lack of commitment.

The current situation forced everyone to move into a fully remote working model, unless there were legal obstacles. The logistics and security reasons were mostly ironed out in the first few weeks, to enable the smooth running of the show.

Now with the model proven, companies are realising the potential cost savings that could be achieved due to reduced infrastructure, if implemented on a permanent basis. For the society in general, it has many positive indications like less travel so consequently less pollution, etc.

Twitter and Facebook have already offered their staff the option to work remotely on a permanent basis and expect a vast majority to take up this offer. TCS has announced it plans to retain this model, with only 25 per cent of the workforce in office at any given time to achieve 100 per cent productivity. They are proving to be the industry bellwethers and others will follow suit.

On the surface of it, this looks like a great move. The companies benefit on reduced infrastructure cost, being able to tap into a previously location constrained talent pool and savings from reduced salaries.

Overall people may move out of cities to more peaceful towns. Property prices and associated services will be negatively affected in large cities, especially like Bangalore which are heavily reliant on IT, as money will move to smaller cities. The overcrowded city resources may breathe a sigh of relief.

Now, let us keep these side-effects aside and focus on what will be the consequence for the employees, if done on a permanent basis.

The first thing that springs to mind is people will have a great work life balance.

Can we take a quick poll please? Let me guess, the result will be a resounding No. Most people are currently struggling to cope at home, what with increased housework and mental fatigue. Those living alone and leading a virtual life now, are desperate to go back to having in-person interactions and this cannot be just with family.

Men feel overloaded with responsibilities from being available for housework and child care, they did not even realise existed. Women however are currently doing a "double-double shift",[3] as perfectly said by Sheryl Sandberg, COO of Facebook. She says, women who work full-time usually do a double shift as

---

3   https://fortune.com/2020/05/07/coronavirus-women-sheryl-sandberg-lean-in-employers-covid-19/

they do office work and are also responsible for housework and child care. Now they have to take up home schooling and caring for the sick and the elderly. She has asked employers to step in and help. Even with children back in school and the pandemic over, the constant "double shift", with no physical and mental respite, will slowly break them. They will never be able to switch out of either home or office.

What if both you and your partner work from home permanently? Firstly, do you have the physical space and environment needed for it? Secondly, will you be able to clearly compartmentalise work and home or end up doing more of both? Men will struggle but let us be honest, with the woman being at home the demands on her will be endless. The expectation to spare 15 minutes to cook a quick lunch/serve meal/ make tea, etc will exist. In case they fail, the taunts of being incapable of planning your day will follow. The accepted social norm is, you cannot disturb a man if he is working but the same does not hold true for a woman.

The second benefit could be that people can move to cheaper destinations and save. This may be true to some extent, as the cost of living will also be less, at least initially.

However, the fat salaries will be replaced by more realistic numbers, suitable to the location you pick. Mark Zuckerberg was upfront that the salaries will be adjusted to the cost of living of the place you choose and if found lying, the consequences will be severe. Consequently, your purchasing power may reduce, compared to your city peers. Combined with rising prices in towns due to increased demand, the expected savings will nosedive. The quality of associated services like education and medical facilities may vary too. Along with this the availability of a larger talent pool will drive down current salaries.

Finally, the greatest benefit may be opening up opportunities for a location constrained talent pool.

It would help people find jobs without leaving their hometowns. It may reduce the daily flow of thousands to the already congested cities. The opportunity of being able to work and earn while being able to fulfil family responsibilities and location constraints will be a blessing for some people. It may even trigger a move back to a loose model of joint family. The aging parents will be happy to have their children and grandchildren around.

Yet, what of building an independent family unit, away from meddling relatives? What of the dreams of the young students, finally moving to work in a large city? They may experience financial and physical freedom, for the first time. The exposure gives them confidence, builds their character and expands their friend list too. So, not everyone will be amenable to this model.

Moreover, will complete remote working not lead to increased social segregation? The work place is a great equaliser and I personally believe it is the one place where we are forced to meet a diverse crowd, who we have not inherently chosen due to our similarities. To work efficiently we have to suppress our unconscious bias and listen to various viewpoints, professionally and sometimes personally, especially over a cup of coffee or watercooler chatter. It broadens our minds horizon.

While this may adversely affect everyone, again women will be the worst hit by it. It may result in some of them being further pushed into a controlled and isolated environment under the guise of having financial independence. They may never be able to step outside the confines of their houses to meet other people, to get exposure to other worlds or alternative views, away from prying eyes and ears.

The list of pros and cons with their effects are many. Overall, it may prove to be a positive move, if everyone works towards a system with the right checks and balances in place.

The employees will need to prioritise their needs. They will have to manage the social front and set some expectations and boundaries at home. This may even result in a few changes to their current social fabric itself.

However, the onus of providing structure and support, would lie on the employer too. They would have to ensure the system considers the requests of each person regarding location, and not blindly force people. Easy access to support could be made available, as people do not have the benefit of asking colleagues casually or seeing the distress or worry on somebody's face and offering to help. The culture of openness or unscripted meetings could replace the benefits of in-person chats too. I am sure there are enough experts to guide them.

Ultimately it will be a boon for some and a bane for others but if we aim to make it a boon for the majority and inclusive of the needs for the minority, then it is a model worth fighting for.

Earth provides enough to satisfy every man's need, but not every man's greed.

– Mahatma Gandhi

22. Let Us Comfort Earth in the Warmth of our Cotton-Filled Quilts!

It is autumn and the nights are getting colder so time to swap out the light blanket for a thick duvet. Given that it had not been washed since last year's use, I took it to the dry cleaner. He queried whether I really wanted it washed as the cost was almost as much as buying a new one, if not more. Apparently, the trend now is to use and throw away a duvet every year, rather than go through the cost and hassle of storing and washing it. A classic case of consumerism, don't you think?

I remember my childhood days, when we used to have cotton-filled quilts. A man used to come around on a bicycle in late autumn to remove the cotton and fluff it up, ready for the winter. We have progressed from those cumbersome cotton quilts to lighter and warmer duvets or quilts, thanks to technology. However, the same technology which has reduced cost and increased our affordability, has made us move away from reusing things to a use and throw model, all in the name of convenience.

Have we become lazier, is it about showing off affordability or mere wish for change, I am not sure? Whatever the reason, be it ease, trends or just because we can, this consumerism has driven us to over exploiting our one home, earth.

Rapid progress in medicine and agriculture production, among other things, led to a sharp increase in the world population especially over the last century. This in turn put pressure on the earth to provide resources for our sustenance. In addition to this economic development, primarily driven by exploiting our earth, led to over consumption of goods and services, especially in Western countries.

For example, the US which has around 5 per cent of the world population consumes around 24 per cent of the world's energy. As development and wealth flows to other areas of the world so does over consumption of goods. It is seen as a sign of success. At the current rate of population and economic growth, the global resource constraints are visible on the horizon and calling for us to act, now, before it is too late. If the whole world consumes in the same pattern and rate as the US then we will need five earths to cater to it. This is unsustainable in the long run.

Studies say, our best bet lies in trying to live sustainably. While we should focus on green living, recycling and saving the environment of our earth, overall sustainable living is what will help us reduce our carbon footprint and lead to a net zero living.

Sustainable living does not mean sacrificing our quality of life, rather a change in our very lifestyle. It is about making a conscious effort to consume less or repurpose things and try to be as carbon neutral as possible. It can be practised by individuals, businesses and even governments.

Its positive impact can be environmental, social and economic. The broad objectives of sustainable living are to reduce the use of fossil fuel, conserve energy and water, eliminate waste and try to go local.

The benefit of using public transport where possible to reduce the use of fossil fuel are well known. There is a trend of holding politicians and celebrities to account for using private jets unnecessarily and clocking up carbon emission. Some of them even declare the carbon footprint when they release their travel details. It has led to growing global awareness around the issue. At a personal level we could do our bit by combining our daily walk with a trip to the supermarket, look at using a bike or carpooling, instead of driving everywhere to reduce use of fossil fuel.

The next obvious thing would be to save energy and water, so there is enough for everyone. Small things like switching off power to appliances rather than leaving on standby, using energy efficient LED lights, taking advantage of natural light or even using renewable sources of energy like solar panels can make a huge difference. Saving water by using less or using rainwater harvesting are of course well known but rarely practised.

Then there is the case for reducing exploitation of nature for food. The impact is severe and is being felt around the world in the form of Zoonotic diseases like Covid-19, that transmit from animals to humans. The best way to contribute is to eat less meat or go vegan. Going meat free even for one day a week helps make an appreciable difference to the demand and consequently the environment. Buying organic food benefits our health while being kind to the environment. Seasonal and locally produced food is not only nutritious but helps the local economy and also cuts down on the carbon footprint of the food we eat due to the transportation cost. Growing some food in the garden or indoors helps us get fresh food while developing a hobby and even helping us to destress.

In addition to this we should look at using food that has been grown using sustainable methods like using non-polluting chemicals, renewable energy sources and economic efficiencies of water conservation. After all 25 per cent of the world's greenhouse gases are produced directly as a result of crop, animal production and forestry. They apparently use 60 per cent of the land area too. Yet we clear about 50,000 acres of land every day due to new demand. In just the last 40 years around 20 per cent of the Amazon rainforest has been destroyed. This means increased habitat loss, greenhouse emissions, soil erosion and flooding. We are in a precarious situation where any further exploitation would be catastrophic for us and our planet.

We should take a hard look at our consumption pattern too. Buying lasting fashion instead of fast fashion or going for a minimalistic décor could be an option to reduce our urge to buy things. We could borrow, share or rent if it is a one-off use but it needs a change in attitude and social mindset. We could use sustainably produced paper or go paperless, to help save our forests.

Reusing and repurposing things to cut down on our consumption can help make a major dent too. Avoiding food waste, for instance, is something we can easily work towards. Did you know it takes 125 litres of water to grow one apple? It makes us rethink about letting it go to waste doesn't it? Instead of just recycling those bottles, can we try to reuse them first. Take a look at the labels too. Are the clothes using sustainable materials? Do our cosmetics use sustainable palm oil? What about the packaging, is it recycled? Can we buy unpacked stuff? Today most goods have certificates to show sustainability, else a quick google search will provide us the details.

These are some examples of sustainable living but there are many more ways of contributing towards it. Most of them help in reducing our bills too, so there is a financial motivation to do it, if not for the greater good.

Sustainable living is a reflection of the change in mindset and a deliberate drive to place less burden on our earth. Afterall, earth is a finite space so can produce only a finite amount of resources. Sustainable living will enable us to live on the planet, off its resources, in harmony with it. With a population of 7.8 billion and set to reach 10 billion by 2057, it will become a necessity for our survival. It will let us preserve earth for our future generations, so they survive and have a place to call home.

Meanwhile, I may not be even remotely carbon neutral but I will reuse my duvet and the next time I need some towels to wipe or clean stuff, instead of buying posh microfiber dusting clothes or Egyptian cotton towels I will try to reuse my old cotton t-shirts. After all, isn't it classier to care more about our earth and its future than the cuteness of my cleaning towels or a reflection of my affordability?

❖❖❖

A gender-equal society would be one where the word 'gender' does not exist: where everyone can be themselves.

— Gloria Steinem

23. Women Empowerment Needs a Social Revolution of Core Attitude

As we pray to Maa Durga, the symbol of power and wisdom for our health, prosperity and happiness, maybe we should take a few minutes to also think about the women in our lives? After all, they fill our lives with health and happiness and deserve our love, respect and adoration.

Yet, does our society give them the respect and opportunity to prosper as much as a man or try to clip their wings, sometimes unintentionally? I am not speaking of the crimes and atrocities committed against them here but rather about their right to prosper to their full potential and live life as they choose.

Our society tries to cast them into a well-defined path of expectations and behaviour, right from birth. When a girl is born, most parents start with planning her life. In the Western world they dress her in pink clothes and fill her room with princess toys and wallpaper, instead of giving her the chance to choose or reflect her tastes.

Have you seen a baby girl dressed in jeans or trousers? Rarely. Most are dressed in tiny skirts and dresses, to reflect the accepted norms of society. Does a baby really care about the colour or length of her dress or does she want to be just warm and secure? I have seen a grownup man refusing to wear a light pink shirt, worried that he may appear feminine. It reflects the depth of this colour divide etched in our minds that it makes an adult feel insecure about his own masculinity due to the colour of a shirt.

Next come the toys and books. Even the basic rattle has a girl and boy version, so while the girls get pink diamonds and tiara the boys get animals and vehicle shapes. The boys' rooms are decorated with stars and planets, superheroes or other imaginative ideas, whereas the girls' are decorated with princess themes.

The story books reflect these ideas too. From the onset, we are teaching the boys to reach for the stars and be astronauts or go on adventure trips. Meanwhile, we are teaching our girls that they are weak, helpless, trapped and need a man to rescue them or worse they need to be beautiful, wear cool clothes and look good for a prince to fall in love, marry and make them happy. The success of the Disney princess movies and associated goods franchise is testimony to this culture.

We even describe the traits of beauty in these books and films, making little girls feel insecure from an early age. If you tell an impressionable child this is reality how many of them will actually have the courage to defy social norms, peer pressure and go against every unwritten rule to develop their own personality and fulfil their dreams?

This theme continues well into later life. Both boys and girls have a well-defined idea of what their roles are in society and what is expected of them. As teens and then as adults, no wonder they continue building on these ideas and then when we expect them to adopt gender equality, they have a hard time accepting and reflecting it.

A few years ago there was an uproar when a frustrated father posted a picture of the covers of teen magazines *Girl's Life* and *Boy's Life*, side by side, to bring this issue into focus. The *Girl's Life* was filled with tips about hair and fashion while the Boy's Life cover was highlighting "Explore Your Future: Astronaut? Artist? Firefighter? Chef?" It was very sexist and begged the question: what message are we sending to the children?

Some may argue that the magazine just reflected demand. Do you think that girls will refuse to read about other girls' achievements? Will they not be inspired to try their hand at different things if they know it is acceptable and achievable? It is all about normalising things and changing social perceptions for both boys and girls and the media contributes to it in a big way.

It is not just the girls who are affected by it too. A boy reading that magazine cover will assume that girls are only interested in fashion and when they actually see a girl in their class or even later as colleagues, they will subconsciously type cast her, dismiss her achievements or not take her seriously.

This behaviour also feeds from the environment at home. Do we give the women in our house equal opportunity as the men? Are their views sought and respected or is it just limited to food and fashion choices? If not, then why expect the men in the family to respect and be inclusive of women outside the house? If a child grows up seeing his/her father taking all important decisions, with no input from the mother or any women, then the chances of them involving women later on in life, be it at home, office or elsewhere will be very slim.

If women always sacrifice their careers for a man's, at home, then is it any wonder that men think it is acceptable to get priority over a woman at office, just by virtue of being a male? If we do not have female equality at home, why expect it at work or in the society?

If you want the women in your life to be treated right outside, please be mindful of how you treat them yourself, for that is what will drive her expectations of herself, of people and their behaviour towards her.

Prejudice begins at home; from the day children are born. If we want to empower women and bring in true equality, to let them develop into the best they can be, we need to begin relooking at our mindset right from the start. Our small actions, of trying to typecast our sons and daughters, as early as babies, can sow the seeds for an unequal society.

The path towards women's empowerment and equality begins early and at home. A single decision of buying a ball instead of a doll for a girl or a cooking set instead of a bat for a boy may have a major repercussion on them. Who knows the girl may grow up to play cricket and the boy may grow into a top chef?

So, the next time you want to buy something for a baby, please think about the message you want to convey to them and choose carefully. Give them the gift of choice and open up their world to equal opportunity, the society will follow.

The essence of air transport is speed, and speed is unfortunately one of the most expensive commodities in the world, principally because of the disproportionate amount of the power required to achieve high speed and to lift loads thousands of feet into the air. This is strikingly illustrated by the fact that while an average cargo ship, freight train and transport aeroplane are each equipped with engines totalling about 2,500 H.P., the ship can carry a load of about 7,000 tons, the train 800 tons and the plane only two and a half tons.

- – J. R. D. Tata

24. Hyperloop: A New Mode of Mass Transportation after a Century

The Virgin Hyperloop had its first passenger test this week. Exciting times! As I watched the video of Virgin Hyperloop's Co-Founder and Chief Technology Officer Josh Giegel and Director of Passenger Experience Sara Luchian carry out the first test ride at the DevLoop site in the Nevada desert, I wondered if this is going to be our future mode of public transportation or will it be consigned to the annals of history as an achievable yet unviable option?

Hyperloop is the first mass transportation system to be tested in over 100 years, the last of course being the airplane in the early part of the last century. It was publicly mentioned by Elon Musk in 2012 with the conceptual details published in 2013. Ever the visionary, he and his company SpaceX, basically "open-sourced" it by sharing the details of the technology, for they wanted people to collectively help build the fifth mode of transportation for humanity.

The name Hyperloop was chosen because it travels in a loop at hyper speeds. The word mark "*HYPERLOOP*", applicable to "high-speed transportation of goods in tubes" was issued to SpaceX on April 4, 2017, as per US Patent and Trademark Office.

The fundamental concept is based on the ability of objects to travel at hypersonic speeds, when there is minimal friction. Giant low-pressure tubes, where almost all air has been removed, are constructed either above or below the ground, to create a low friction environment. Then a pod or capsule, containing passengers or for that matter goods, is able to travel within it at high speeds. However, to further reduce friction and improve efficiency, the pod uses magnetic levitation and floats through the tube which results in it achieving speeds of around 700 miles per hour or over.

To put this in context, it will allow us to travel from Bhubaneswar to New Delhi in just over an hour. So, you could arguably travel to New Delhi for a meeting in the morning and be back by evening, faster than a flight. It is a revolutionary technology indeed.

The benefit is not limited to just hyper speeds though. It has no direct emission at all and very low power consumption, making it environmentally friendly. In addition to this, it is enclosed, so works independent of weather conditions and is safe to travel at all times. As the system is centrally controlled there is no scope of traffic jams or collisions. In this case, it is similar to the current flight paths but safer. It has the ability to store energy, so a power failure does not affect it.

Another company working on Hyperloop, Architectural Studio MAD, has even designed a solar powered Hyperloop which is built on raised walkways with green spaces. They want to transform the cityscape into a blend of an extremely efficient mass transportation system on raised pylons, with parks and nature walks embedded alongside and underneath the tubes. It seems like an answer to the endless woes of pollution, environmental impact, traffic and travel time.

An indirect impact of using hyperloop would be the irrelevance of distance for communities. In expensive cities like London and New York, the cost of living is a major factor along with space. If people can travel from as far as Edinburgh to London in 30 minutes, they can live anywhere within a few hundred mile radius and yet commute to work. It will vastly improve the quality of life and reduce the cost of living for everyone.

However, this is a futuristic technology. Although the test ride has proven its potential, it is still a far cry from becoming reality. The current cost of development is exorbitant which will initially restrict its use to short distance high traffic routes, say between New York and Washington DC. In fact, the government of Maharashtra has already approved plans for Virgin Hyperloop One's first hyperloop line to be built between Mumbai and Pune, with a travel time of around 35 mins.

Like any new tech, widespread use will drive down the cost and gradually expand its reach. All this is still a few years away with the first commercial use being forecasted in five to ten years. In the grand scheme of things that is not a long wait.

Meanwhile, companies have to take into account the criticism and risks associated with its implementation. There is the initial high cost and technological challenges to contend with. A genuine concern is the footprint of the network of tubes and their impact on the environment. Unlike roads and rail, they cannot be sculpted to sympathetically match the landscape, rather the landscape needs to be sculpted to its strict scientific needs, as of now. The feasibility and environmental impact of this, outside test conditions, is unknown and may prove to be its undoing.

Then there is the very resistance to change itself. Critics cite the fear and discomfort of people to travel in windowless tubes at extreme speeds but even today we have people who are afraid of flying. Well, I confess to being afraid of riding a horse, so I would have struggled to travel in ancient times.

Whatever the difficulties, the mechanics of it will be ironed out over time. This technology has the capability to transform the way people and communities live and work. It is based on present-day technology for our modern fast paced lifestyles. It has the ability to help solve many of our current global issues like the environmental impact due to emissions from fossil fuels and other lifestyle choices.

It has been a long wait for a new mode of public transportation, suitable for the requirement of contemporary times. Hyperloop could be the answer to it.

❖❖❖

We ourselves feel that what we are doing is just a drop in the ocean. But the ocean would be less because of that missing drop.

- – Mother Teresa

25. Your 1/12th Teaspoon of Honey Matters! Make it Count

I was sorting out my waste diligently when I encountered some thermocol sheets. Unsure of where it was meant to go, the landfill or recycling bin, I requested someone to google it, on account of my hands being dirty. Their response flabbergasted me. "How does it matter? Just stick it in the recycling bin", they said.

It made me pause and ponder on how it did matter actually? If I put it in the recycling bin incorrectly the whole lot would get contaminated and would never get recycled. Yes, in the grand scheme of things one bin may look insignificant but imagine if everyone did so then hardly anything would ever get recycled, ultimately leading to a big impact on the environment. However, as with other things in life, we believe our actions are so small and insignificant compared to the sheer magnitude of the task that we think it does not matter. Little do we realise that each individual and their action is a tiny drop that fills the ocean.

When was the last time you felt powerless, felt inconsequential? Given the current state of the world, it was most likely yesterday, today or at least very recently. With a population of 7.8 billion on the surface of the earth, a lone individual is like a bee in a hive, one of the multitudes.

We feel we have no power to make any material change to the world around us, other than complain of course. We believe we are not the leader of a country, a decision-maker in a social media or media business or in any position of power that own small actions or decisions can make even a dent when in fact the power does lie in us, the public. In today's world power lies in numbers and in the domino effect created by those numbers and we make up the numbers.

Most of the time the massive scale of a problem deters us from taking action. Like thinking that global warming and climate change is so massive a problem and with the best and smartest brains not being able to solve it, what can I do about it? Well we are the very reason they cannot solve it, as we do not listen and assume my one plastic bag or one bottle will hardly make a difference. Imagine if one fine day all of us, all 7 billion of us decided to stop using plastic bottles and bags, the problem will go away instantly. If the world population stopped eating meat for one day the effect on climate change would be dramatic, reducing carbon emission by double digits.

In the current case of the pandemic, we can neither develop a vaccine on our own nor eradicate the virus and bring things back to normalcy. However, we can follow the guidance set by experts and stop its spread. Most of us have all seen the message about the candle that stepped away saved the rest of the world. Our two cents will prevent us from being added to or adding others to the Covid positive list.

Let us take social change as another example. We, the public, complain about equality, unfairness or even women's rights. We complain about the wrong candidate being selected in an election when he won by a majority of a few thousand votes, well were we one of the few thousand who did not go to vote for the right candidate? We complain of harassment of women in public spaces. Did we step up to protest or help when someone was being harassed or did we turn a blind eye to it?

Research shows that people tend to help others less in crowded places as they own less distributed responsibility for their actions and tend to think someone else will do it. Meanwhile, if alone, they will make an effort to actually be the one helping as they are solely responsible for it. It just shows that people do want to contribute but we are wired to think we are nonentities in a crowd and our actions do not matter when in reality that is when it matters most, as that is when we can truly bring about change.

However, taking action needs commitment and will cost us time, effort and may be some money. For example, recycling diligently takes time and effort. I do have to invest in buying a reusable coffee cup and more importantly remember to carry it for my takeaway coffee, whereas the single use disposable cup is free and convenient. Meanwhile, did you know that 16 billion single use paper cups are consumed for coffee every single year, which leads to 6.5 million trees cut down, 4 billion gallons of water going to waste, and enough energy to power 54,000 homes for a year also goes to waste? So, if all of us carried our own cups, we would be making a massive difference.

Of course, we do need to understand the larger issue, take a stand based on our ideology, make an effort to understand what we can do to help and only then do our bit.

The best example of this would be the very honeybee we compared ourselves to earlier. Beekeeper Marianne Gee, who lives in Ottawa, Canada gave a lovely TED talk where she spoke of the honeybees. They have around six weeks to live and they spend it selflessly collecting honey, so their species can survive. They do not spend time over thinking the big picture, rather just get on with doing their bit. In their entire lifetime they collect about $1/12^{th}$ of a teaspoon of honey but collectively the hive is able to make hundreds of kilos of honey.

Our tendency to think of the larger picture makes us feel we are insignificant. Instead we need to chip away at the issue without over thinking about the big picture and our contribution will add up and make a difference.

We have the capability to bring about change collectively, by working individually. Perhaps it is time we recognise our power and use it to bring about some good, some much needed changes in our society, by taking a stand and contributing our share of honey.

Our 1/12th teaspoon honey counts! Together we can bring about change.

Acknowledgement

This book wouldn't have been possible without the support and encouragement of Punya Prava Rath, editor of Odishabytes. It all started with a request for an article on life during lockdown, which then led to many more being written.

I would like to thank my parents for inspiring me, for reading each essay diligently and passing bouquets or brickbats.

My gratitude to Mr. Sampad Mohapatra for his initial review and advice, which helped me take my first step on this journey.

Special thanks my family and friends for putting up with my absences, reading my articles with patience, providing feedback where appropriate and encouraging me to keep writing.

Finally, my sincere thanks to my publisher Sudarshan Kcherry Sir for helping convert my vision into a reality.

9 789390 588039